# DEERPARK

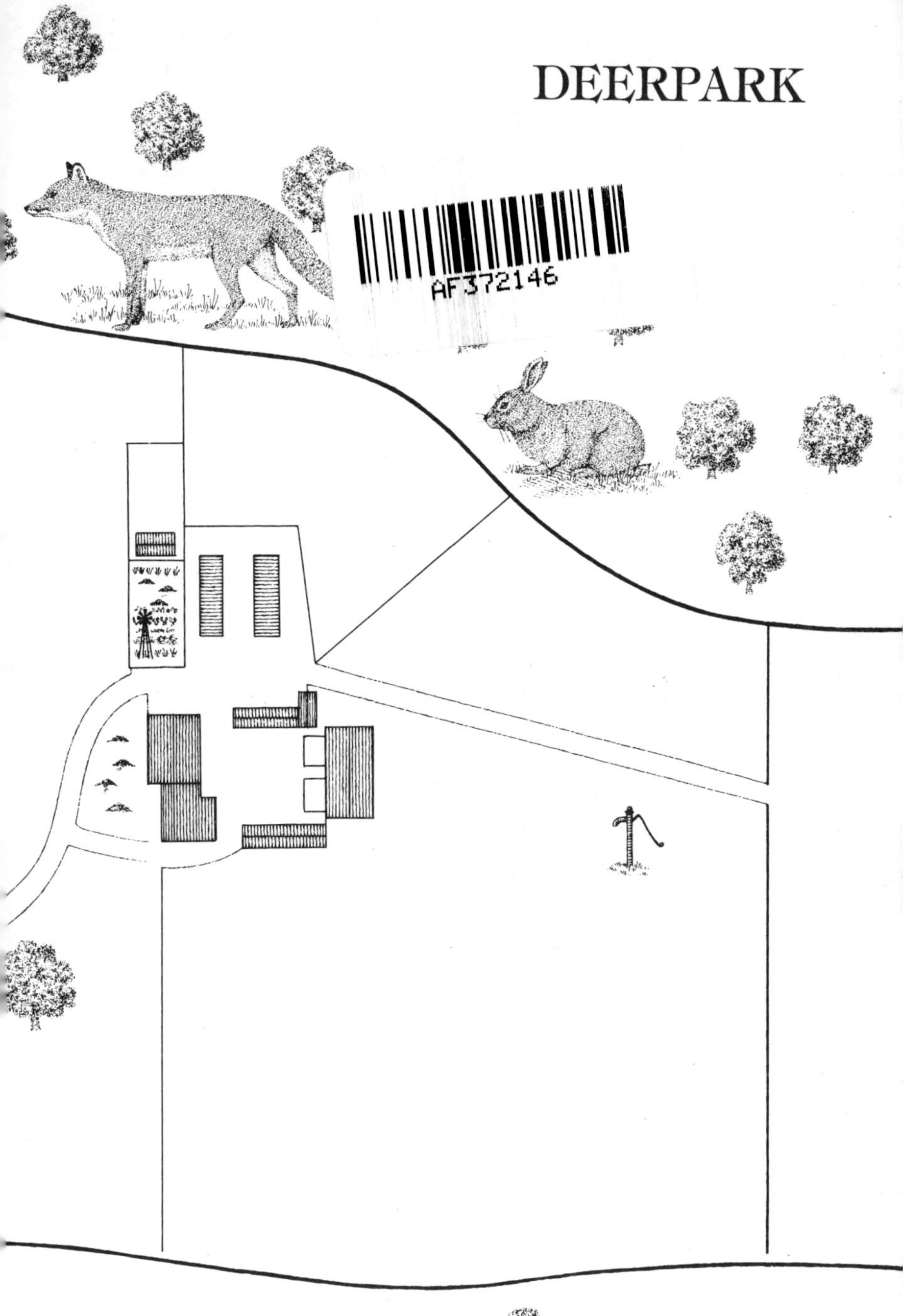

# HOLIDAY FARM

*By the same author*

THE  GREAT  DROUGHT  OF  1976

# HOLIDAY FARM
# Evelyn Cox

## Illustrations by Rodney Shackell

HODDER AND STOUGHTON

LONDON SYDNEY AUCKLAND TORONTO

British Library Cataloguing in Publication Data
Cox, Evelyn
  Holiday Farm
  1. Farms—Recreational use—England—Herefordshire
  (Hereford and Worcester)
  I. Title
  647'.94424'4        TX910.G7

  ISBN 0 340 27835 8



Hodder and Stoughton Editorial Office: 47 Bedford Square, London WC1B 3DP.

# Author's Note

You will not find the village Micklebury on an Ordnance Survey map nor will you find Deerpark Farm listed in the English Tourist Board's *Where to Stay* guides. The interests of places and people are sometimes best served by their remaining anonymous. For the same reason I have not described actual individuals in our locality, but have created a series of characters who do not portray any living men or women but who do, I believe, reflect the type of people who shared our lives during this period. The guests described in the book are composite characters.

# Contents

# The end of a dream

Once—it seems light years away, but it was in the days before the summer season of 1977—my family led a normal life. Or as normal a life as any farming family can lead. My husband, Tom, and I and our eighteen-month-old son, Anthony, had a home we could call our own: we ate regular meals seated at the kitchen table, with only the odd interruption; we slept in proper beds; sometimes we even went out for the evening, or had friends to stay.

All that has changed. Now every Saturday afternoon, from the first brave April days until the dying autumn evenings at the end of October, sees me fiddling with the flowers in the front garden as I wait to welcome the latest batch of holidaymakers who will take over our farmhouse for the following week. We eat our meals in haste; we sleep on a variety of camp beds and 'put-you-up' contraptions, moving around from bedrooms to boxrooms in the attic. If we want a bath, it is quite likely that the bathroom will be occupied by someone washing stockings in the washbasin. For seven months of the year we step aside and let strangers have the run of the greater part of the house. Some are difficult and grumpy; a few are outright ghastly—people who arrive back in the middle of the night fighting drunk, or children who smash up my son's toys. But most, thank goodness, are warm-hearted, friendly and appreciative. Living cheek by jowl with people we have never met before has been an extraordinary experience. There have been hilarious moments as well as shudderingly embarrassing incidents. And, most of all, we have had a fascinating glimpse of life as seen from the other side of the serving hatch.

It all began one warm March day. I was weeding the vegetable garden, churning over in my mind the apparently insoluble problem of how to make a living from our forty-acre livestock farm in the depths of the Herefordshire countryside. We were at the start of spring in the year that followed the great drought of 1976. The eighteen months of abnormally dry weather, which had culminated in the nightmare summer of the drought, had given way in September to six months of deluge. Our small farm, dependent as it was on two wells and a dew pond, all of which went dry, had felt the fullest impact of the drought. When the rains at last came in September we were profoundly thankful. But when they not only came, but stayed right through the winter into the New Year, they became literally too much of a good thing. We found ourselves unable to get on with one essential task after another. In particular we could not get at that key job on a livestock farm, spreading the muck from the byres and barns on to the fields to fertilise them for a new season.

And we needed that fertility. The great drought had meant not only physical hardship for my husband and myself. It had dealt us a severe financial blow. We had had to pay out money to have water carted in for ourselves and our stock, whilst the meagre grass had meant less weight on our cattle and lower prices for them when they were sold in the autumn. As the rain streamed down our windows that winter and we worked over the farm accounts for the year, one fact stared us in the face. Our smallholding venture, which we had begun three years before, was doomed unless we could, during the next spring and summer, find some way of making extra money and making it quickly.

The drought was only the latest of a series of blows which had hit British agriculture since, in the autumn of 1973, we had moved into Deerpark Farm in mid-Herefordshire. At that time British farming was riding high, with buoyant livestock prices and with reasonable fuel and feeding stuff costs. We knew that forty acres was a very small farm indeed, but my husband, a former show-jump rider and trainer, had a specialist line—the rearing and training of horses for show jumping, eventing and hunting—with which to supplement our other farming income. The horse world was, at that time, booming and profitable. If we buttressed our horse business by running beef cattle and a flock of breeding ewes, and by growing as much of our own food as possible, we believed we could at least make ends meet. Our forty acres were some of the most fertile in Britain, broad acres of rich reddish-brown Herefordshire soil, with a good permanent pasture that promised good hay crops. The farm house was primitive, with stone-flagged floors, and a yard that looked, even in that dry winter, as if it could become a midden once the rains came (as indeed it did).

If we repaired and improved the house ourselves and put such spare capital as we had into turning some of the farm buildings into loose boxes for the horses, there seemed a reasonable chance that we could make a go of things. And we would be doing that in surroundings of real beauty, which was a reward in itself. We were three quarters of a mile from the nearest village, Micklebury, up our own farm road. The whole farm was ringed with trees—said to have been planted by Capability Brown when this was part of a large estate—lines of tall beech, oak and ash. From the upper windows of the house the Malvern Hills were a faint, low tracery to the south-east;

to the north stood Clee Hill, only slightly spoilt by the white dome of its radar station; to the west, through the trees of a big beech wood, could be glimpsed the mountains of Wales. Capability Brown's handsome oaks, alternating with one fine fir tree and the broken but lovely shape of a sweet chestnut, were full grown and strong. A pool, said to be a dew pond, had been carved out of the rock on the highest point of the fields. An iron windmill which had once drawn water from the well stood, it is true, at a crazy angle, like a metal leaning tower of Pisa; the old vegetable garden was a mass of couch grass and bindweed; the hedges were ragged, and every building needed some repair and a lot of paint. But, set apart on its small plateau, Deerpark cried out to be used, not only as a farm but as a home. We decided to risk all we had, and use it in just that way.

So in the lovely Indian summer of 1973 we took the plunge, got in at the head of the mad scramble of would-be buyers as Deerpark was put on the market, and set about making a reality of our dreams. Our first task was to get the buildings into some sort of shape. What had been listed as 'loose boxes, calf sheds and yearling pens' were in reality a shanty town of sheds clad with rotting timber patched with rusty corrugated iron. With the aid of some second-hand timber, which had once formed the roof of Hereford's munitions factory, we turned these into two lines of loose boxes, facing each other across the farmyard, comprising separate, strong warm units of stabling. The vast corrugated-iron roof of the French barn was transformed until it looked like new under a liberal application of black bitumastic paint. The massive oak beams and supports of the barn itself needed little attention. They too had been recycled in their day, from one of the great sailing ships in the nineteenth century. The wood is heart of oak, and should last a thousand years. But we gave the barn new outside walls, concrete

floors, and some additional gates, and so equipped ourselves with covered accommodation for about thirty-five
cattle during the long winter months.

Our greatest achievement, however, was to conquer
the mire in the middle of the farmyard. This yard, or, to
be more precise, this space between the buildings, was
full of grass, stones, wild barley and bits of old pipe,
rusty saucepans, broken machinery and other scrap. By
mid-January it had become a lagoon of mud and manure
which was four feet deep in places, and which stretched
from the back door of the house across to the narrow
concrete pathways along the edge of the buildings. Along
these pathways we had to carry the bales of fodder, or to
push muck-laden wheelbarrows from the loose boxes. It
was like skirting the slippery edges of a municipal swimming pool—with the added hazard that a true midden
awaited you if you did slip. Five hundred tons of stone
had to be tipped into the space, and set into position
before we could change this. But in the end we had
banished the mud and muck for ever, and in their place
was a firm even surface which stood up to the heaviest
rain and snows of the winter, and which looked like a
college quadrangle with farm buildings on three sides,
and the back of the house covering much of the fourth.

In such time as we could spare from looking after the
animals and rebuilding their quarters we reorganised and
redecorated the house. Our first task was to provide a
proper scullery. For two months I had no kitchen sink,
only a bucket for the washing up. But we turned the
corrugated-iron wash-house which had been built on to
the rear of the kitchen into a solid scullery, equipped it
with a stainless-steel sink, and an electric cooker, a big
farm refrigerator and a washing-machine. The cooker
was a support and a reserve for the coal-fired Aga which
stood against one wall of the kitchen, that room which,
with its big deal table, is the heart of every true farmhouse.

I had many skills to learn—how to glaze, to sweep chimneys, to clean out drainpipes. There was more to self-sufficiency than I had ever imagined. But gradually from the mess our home emerged. We redecorated all five bedrooms—four in the main part of the house, plus one small but attractive attic bedroom above the kitchen, reached by a sheer ladder-like stairway. We transformed the feel of the place by knocking down a dividing wall between the old front parlour and a store room to its rear, so producing a sitting room which ran from the front of the house to the back, with windows on three sides. This gave what had seemed a pokey and cramped house a new sense of spaciousness.

Into the barns around the house we placed the horse box and caravan which formed part of the essential equipment of a show jumper, and such agricultural machinery as we possessed. With us moved in what seemed a virtual Noah's Ark of animals—horses and calves, guard dogs, sheep dogs, terriers. Our first flock of sheep, purchased at Gloucester Market, grazed on the front pastures. From somewhere the first of our ever changing but ever present population of cats appeared. So we settled down to prove to ourselves (and to the bank manager) that we could make our way in this outpost of England.

Then came, in quick succession, the quadrupling of oil prices, the three-day week, the fall of the Heath government, and months of uncertainty about agricultural policy, as Westminster dithered about whether to stay in the Common Market. All of this precipitated British farming into its worst depression since the war. The livestock market in particular crumbled. We could no longer afford to buy in hay from other farms, but would have to grow our own. This meant that we must reduce the amount of stock we carried and so, in 1975, we sold off our flock of sheep. We had done reasonably well with them, averaging one point eight lambs per ewe. But they had made huge demands on our time and energies. Sheep are deceptive animals. Seen over the hedgerow, as you drive along a country road, ewes and lambs look such easy animals to rear, able to live out in the winter, needing few special feeds. In practice they call for incessant attention, being highly susceptible to disease and needing not merely shepherding but nursing. So we decided to concentrate on cattle and horses.

The horse market was the next to be undermined. We had our first clear sign of this when we experienced great difficulty in selling a hunter of a type which was usually very much in demand.

Jimmy Brown was not merely a horse with a straightforward name, but a good, straightforward hunter. In normal times we would have found a new home for him very quickly. But no one, it seemed, wanted to buy hunters. So we turned him out to grass in the front pasture, through which the road runs to the farmhouse. There he began to display an infuriating characteristic. When we drove down the road Jimmy Brown would often be standing on it, and he stood his ground. No amount of revving the engine or tooting the horn would budge him, even shouts and arm waving produced interest but no movement. One day as I got back in the passenger seat, after grabbing Jimmy Brown by his forelock and leading him away, I said to Tom: "That's not a hunter. He's a ruddy police horse!"

"You've got something there," Tom exclaimed. "We'll sell him as a police horse. I'll ring the mounted police people I met last year at the Horse of the Year Show."

So Jimmy Brown ended up not as a hunter galloping after foxes in the shires, but as a police horse controlling football crowds in a North Midlands industrial town. I thought I caught a glimpse of him once on a news film, shepherding along a throng of youths with multi-coloured scarves and sullen expressions. He also achieved national fame in classes for the mounted police at horse shows, proving to be particularly outstanding in tent-pegging competitions.

The other aspects of the horse trade were all in decline. Not only did there seem to be no market for hunters or show jumpers, there was no demand either for the breaking or schooling of horses and very little for keeping horses at livery. Indeed the main demand for horses was not for animals to ride, but for animals to slaughter. The grisly fact became gradually clear that at the monthly horse sales in Hereford, most of the horses and ponies which came up for sale were being purchased for meat. This was true all over the country. It was estimated that ninety-five per cent of all native ponies changing hands at auctions were destined for the continental butchers' slabs.

The scene in our local sale ring appeared innocuous enough to those who were unaware of the pitiful reality of the horse world under the impact of inflation and of the undervalued green pound, with its debilitating influence on all country life. The benches of the amphitheatre of the ring were full of horse owners and other equine enthusiasts. There were young women in headscarves, children with pony club badges, old bow-legged men in breeches. But at the side of the sale ring itself was a very different group of people, formed by five prosperous men dressed in smart cavalry twill trousers and tweed jackets. They looked very much at home and laughed and joked amongst themselves. They did most of the bidding and bought most of the horses. They were the horse slaughterers buying up animals for meat to be exported to Belgium.

For a few of the horses the slaughterhouse came as a merciful release. Starved and riddled as they were with parasites after a winter on bare fields, life could offer them little. But others were well cared-for family ponies: 'Schooled and hunted all winter. Good in traffic,' said the catalogue. Or, 'Genuine all-round family pony. Good hunter and used to all pony club activities. Highly recommended and fully warranted.' And another: 'Perfect child's first pony. Been with family since a two-year-old. Only for sale as owner outgrown.'

Outside the sale ring under the chestnut trees, softly green with young buds, the owners of the outgrown were putting the ponies through their paces. This rarely made any difference to their fate. Occasionally a bidder in the stands was seeking a pony to ride, and clinched the sale and provided his name to the auctioneers with a certain amount of blushing and embarrassment. But most of the ponies and horses went to the group by the auctioneer's box, men who were such familiar figures they did not bother with such formalities. It is not the least of the ironies of the Common Market that it has stimulated this British export trade in horse flesh, a product not covered by Common Agricultural Policy regulations, and so able to rise to its true price, which was then higher than the fixed price for prime beef.

These man-made difficulties were bad enough. When the fates produced in 1976 the driest weather ever recorded, followed by the wettest winter of the century, we found ourselves with huge problems on our hands. On the face of it, we seemed doomed to admit failure, and sell.

We worked, like almost all farmers, from year to year on an overdraft from the bank. Because most farm produce, whether arable crops or livestock, is harvested only once a year, farmers need resources to tide themselves over until these harvests are gathered in. The bank overdraft enabled us to buy our calves in the autumn, to purchase feeding stuffs to carry them through the winter, and to help meet other costs like fuel and fertiliser. In the late spring the cattle were turned out to feed through the summer on good Herefordshire grass, until they were sold in the autumn. It was a nice logical system—provided you had enough resources to get through until the autumn cheques came in. If not, you were in trouble. For the bills did not wait till the autumn. The bill for feeding stuffs and for diesel, the vet's bill and the electricity bill, the rates demand, the telephone account and above all the demands for interest on the bank overdraft, all poured in regardless, needing to be paid then and there.

We had to face in that winter after the drought the fact that we would not have the money to get through to the next autumn unless we could find some supplementary source of income. The traditional defence of the small-holder against this problem is for the husband—or the wife—to take on a job outside the farm. This was not open to us. I had a two-year-old baby son who not only tied me to the place, but also prevented me from keeping it going on my own, had my husband got a job outside. The farm needed the labour of both of us. So any new money we generated had to be generated on the farm—and generated within a matter of months, if not weeks. There was not time, for instance, to switch to milking—the quickest cash crop in farming. And in any event our water supply was inadequate to run a milking shed of any size. Pigs and poultry, those other stand-bys of the small farmer, had been even harder hit than had beef farming. On them the new Common Market pricing arrangement bore with particular ferocity. We had to find some other way.

This was the problem which one March afternoon I took off to my favourite spot for contemplation; the vegetable garden.

# A new cash crop

Dilute spring sunshine filtered through the bare branches of the knobbly oaks and the green-budded arms of the ash trees in the wood that guarded the western flank of our farm. Foresters had been felling and hacking and chopping at this thick screen of trees for the past eighteen months and had at last succeeded in thinning the woodland barrier just beyond our boundary fence. I felt as if not just a wind-break but a protection had gone—almost a symbol of the way our financial flank was exposed.

The wood had seemed to absorb and hold the wind which hit it full blast from the Welsh mountains, until not just the trees but the very ground seemed to bend under the strain. Now you could look through the trees and see the Black Mountains rising on the far side of the Marches; mountains that seem to be waiting, watchful, but never threatening or imposing. The countryside stretching across the intervening plain was pale and colourless in the hazy mist; the world was still hibernating. Grass lank and tawny, handfuls of woods and copses dark and barren, all were waiting silently for the first warm sunshine of the new season to prompt that frenzy of growth that bursts on us miraculously each spring.

Nearer at hand some growth was well underway.

Between the neat rows of cauliflowers, spring cabbage and broad beans in the kitchen garden, stretched a green carpet of weeds. Groundsel, red and white dead-nettles, chickweed, wild carrot, ground ivy, couch grass, all competed for space. I was tackling the weeds in amongst rows of cabbages in the lee of the redundant, leaning windmill that tops our well. With me was Doreen, an Australian girl who had been helping us with the horses. She was attacking the invasion around the onion shoots. She did so with gusto. Weeds were flying into her bucket and she was singing her favourite song—'Tie Me Kangaroo Down Sport'—while the windmill beat time, revolving crazily and uselessly in the breeze.

Weeding is both a satisfying and contemplative job. There is the satisfaction of reducing the green chaos to neat rows of shoots with soft brown earth between, and, being repetitive, it leaves your mind free to think. I contemplated the cauliflowers with some care. We had a good crop of about twenty, but they had been a lot of work. I had fought to keep the seedlings alive in the dry weather, and had then netted them against the wheeling, raiding pigeons. Now if cauliflowers were worth the work invested in them, I mused, then perhaps through some form of market gardening we could make some money. But, like everything connected with selling produce from a farm, the monetary rewards were rotten. We had enough food in the garden to feed an army—well perhaps not an army, but at least another couple of families. But to market it would be prohibitively expensive. Then the seed of an idea began to germinate in my mind. We produced not only all our own vegetables, but our own eggs, milk and lamb. We had two spare bedrooms and an extra living room. Perhaps if we could not make money from animals in our farm buildings we could try making it from people in our farmhouse. Instead of selling our produce at very little profit off the farm, we should feed some of it to holidaymakers, at a reasonable profit, here on the farm.

I did some quick mental calculations. What did guest houses charge for bed, breakfast and evening meal nowadays? Perhaps as much as £4 or £5 a night. We had a spare double room and a spare single room. We might be able to make anything from £60 to £100 a week. That was the sort of money we needed.

"Tom! Tom!" I yelled, "I think I've got the answer." But as I rushed onto the yard to find my husband, my first euphoria was already receding. I began to see some serious snags. There were no washbasins in the bedrooms and surely people nowadays expected not only washbasins but private showers? We had only one bathroom in the whole house and the only lavatory was in it. The immersion heater only did one bath an hour. What if two people wanted a morning bath? There would not be enough water for both of them and meanwhile no one else would be able to get to the lavatory. Then there was the road. It was no route for the ordinary light family car. Whole stretches of it had subsided during the appallingly wet winter, and even our indefatigable postman had been unable to drive up it for the past month.

Somewhat deflated, I outlined my idea to Tom. He was encouraging: "The bathroom is perfectly all right. People who stay in farmhouses don't expect hotel standards. They want a decent bed, good food and somewhere they can have a wash and a shave. We'll fix the road up as best we can."

The next step was a phone call to the local tourist board. They reassured me about the adequacy of our washing arrangements. In theory the lavatory should be separate, but the rules are bent where farmhouses and bed and breakfast establishments are concerned. The important rule was that guests should have access to the bathroom at reasonable times and should not be charged extra for baths. I began to have an inkling of the ins and outs of the business. (Charge extra for baths! I thought they only did that in youth hostels in Greece.) A most helpful man told me what sort of food people would expect, where to advertise for bookings, and what facilities we should provide to attract people—mainly a colour television. He also promised to send me a list of farmhouses in the area so I could decide what was the going rate for our type of place.

"There are only two things you have *got* to do," he added. "Tell the VAT office if you are registered, because you will have to charge VAT, and extend your farm insurance to cover paying guests. Good luck, and welcome to the business."

The post brought the promised reading matter. Studying the rates at other farmhouses we decided to charge £5 a night for bed, breakfast and evening meal, or £32 for a full week. A booklet from the Ministry of Agriculture outlined the accepted standards for such things as the size of bedrooms, and the furniture that should be in them. Towards the end it sounded a cautionary note: 'Farmers' wives may find they are working an eighteen-hour day.' My enthusiasm was not dented. It was a possible way to earn money, a job I could do on the farm with my two-year-old son Anthony, at my heels. Better than pulling rhubarb at 87p an hour any day.

It was left to the Bakers, the proprietors of the Old Rectory guest house in Micklebury, to fill us in about the snags. Over a drink in our living room, shortly to be metamorphosed into 'The Lounge', Jill and Harry Baker gave us the benefit of their experience of ten years in the holiday trade.

"First of all," said Harry, "you want to get some notices up. You want one outside saying 'Cars and their contents are parked at owners' risk.' I don't know how you stand in common law with that but it does stop the chap who tries it on by saying, 'Your dog jumped all over my paintwork.'"

"People don't do that sort of thing, do they?" I asked.

"You get all sorts coming on holiday. Most people are no trouble but a few don't think they've had a good time unless they've made life absolute hell for everybody," replied Harry.

"Another thing you probably haven't thought of is your farm animals." Jill Baker made a helpless gesture. "Honestly, people with animals. We have a notice in the bedrooms saying only people used to animals should approach them, and that on no account should any animals be fed. They feed them anything. Two years ago one of the horses went down with colic after someone had given him their lunch of ham sandwiches. And they will get up behind the horses shouting 'horsey! horsey!' and then do their nut because the horse kicks out."

I was full of ideas about serving home-made soups and special steak and kidney pies. Jill Baker discouraged me with a brief outline of our national tastes: "No made-up dishes like casseroles or steak and kidney pies. People like roasts and grills with no sauces and ordinary vegetables like peas, beans and occasionally carrots. Things you and I may love like broccoli and spring cabbage come straight back to the kitchen untouched. It's the same with lovely sauces you've spent hours slaving over. We had some children last week who had never seen a baked potato before."

Harry added his contribution: "Plenty of tomato sauce, absolutely masses of it. HP sauce, Worcester sauce, and of course gallons of vinegar for chips. Make sure the table is well away from the wall or they'll have more sauce over that than over their food. And teapots. Mind the spout pours properly. They seem to get tea everywhere too."

"Oh God" I said, "It sounds absolutely awful. What about breakfast?"

Harry had breakfast costed out down to the last cornflake.

"You only want one type of cereal—cornflakes are best because they don't absorb too much milk. And don't give them too large a helping anyway or they'll use too much milk. Then just one variety of juice at a time. Offer a choice and they'll um and arr and change their minds and you will have a fridge full of half-used cartons, all getting a bit stale.

"And while we're on the subject of breakfast, those pre-packed portions of butter and marmalade are more economical. If you give them butter in a dish guests will mess it up and then expect a clean lump at the next meal. As for jars of marmalade; well by the time you've washed out the jar, and they've had the spoon in it and on the tablecloth and some on the wall you might just as well give them the packaged portions."

His wife added: "And don't forget to charge extra for tea and coffee after dinner. Everyone does." She looked at me severely. I got the message.

Tom and I were aghast at the Bakers' description of guest-house gastronomy. We realised that knocking hotels had become an important element in the new national sport of consumerism. But the view from the other side of the serving hatch seemed much more alarming. We thought the Bakers were exaggerating. Time proved they were not. Most of our guests had perfect table manners, but there were a few formidable exceptions. Getting the gravy stains off our living-room wall was to be a major job at the end of our first season.

During the evening we picked the Bakers' brains on everything from what kind of sheets to provide (nylon, deep colours), where to buy furniture (civil service surplus) to how to deal with difficult visitors. Harry explained a common predicament. "We've never had any non-payers but what you get is people booking for a week because they know they won't get in unless they do and then deliberately staying only a couple of days. They claim to have got an urgent message from home and it's: 'Oh dear, how terrible, we're so disappointed, we've been called home.'"

"Now by law you are entitled to two thirds of what they would have paid and don't be too polite to ask for it. It's funny but all the difficult guests we've had always come from the south. People from the north are much more easy going. Southerners are so smooth with their la-di-da voices but are much more likely to quibble about the bill."

"You don't have to tell me what part of the country you and Jill come from," I laughed. "Any other words of warning?"

"No, just remember this." Harry frowned with thought. "Don't fall over yourself trying to do too much for people. This isn't the Great Northern Hotel. You are offering a certain standard of accommodation at a certain price. But some people are never satisfied and if someone is really difficult don't be afraid to show them the door. Also be prepared for the fact that a few people will leave because they don't like it. We had some people last summer who couldn't bear the quiet and left the next day. When it just happens to you it can be a shock. You feel it is not just a guest house but your house they're walking out of. But don't let it worry you; it happens to everyone."

In the months and years ahead the Bakers' words of advice were often to echo in my mind. There were times when I recalled their warnings, comforting myself that the difficulties we encountered afflicted everyone who took summer visitors. But I did wonder at times if Deerpark got more than its fair share.

We went ahead and sent advertisements off to three different periodicals. We set a starting date several weeks ahead so that we could complete our preparations. But the venture that was supposed to solve our financial crisis looked at first to be a non-starter. The first weekend I hung around within earshot of the telephone waiting for a rush of enquiries. Surely, I thought, that cleverly-worded advertisement would at least entice people to ring up. There was not one phone call, not one letter. We started to think the farm holiday business was going to be one further blow to our hopes at Deerpark. But the next weekend we had several enquiries. The first two were women who said they would ring back when they had talked to their husbands. I stayed up until eleven o'clock—the middle of the night in our household—but they never rang back. I was in a terrible state. What on earth had I said to put them off? What had I done wrong? Were we charging too much? It has happened many times since and, though it does not worry me now, I still wonder.

The next two people wanted to come but they needed a place for the following week. I thought of the road so full of potholes, the front hall still without a carpet and the paint peeling off the bedroom ceiling, and so I, sadly, put them off.

"Doesn't anyone want to come when we want them to come?" I lamented to Tom. Just then the phone rang. Could we accommodate five people for Jubilee week. Jubilee week? When on earth was that, I wondered. "Er, just a moment."

I consulted Tom. "Where can we put five people? We can't fit five people in, can we?"

Tom looked at me sternly. "The first thing you've got to learn about any business is never to turn customers away. Two of them can sleep in our room. We'll sleep in the caravan or the kitchen or the lorry if we have to. It's not important."

I took up the phone again. "Yes, we can manage that. Are two double rooms and one single all right?" Yes, it was, and triumphantly we entered our first booking in the diary. I blessed the Queen and her Jubilee. We were under way. Within another week we had had several more successful telephone calls. The reservations were in due course confirmed in writing. We drew a sketch map and had it photostated so that our visitors would start with at least a sporting chance of finding us.

Our next problem was to raise some cash to stock up with food for the guests and with stone for the road. My mother promised us some extra blankets, crockery, chairs and chests of drawers. These items were dispatched immediately by a famous removal firm and were not seen again for many a week. But we still had to finance our enterprise. Our overdraft had gone to its limits to pay for our livestock. Since I was determined that the paying-guest business should pay its way from the outset I did not want to dip into our almost invisible reserves. The only answer was to find something on the farm which we could sell. If we did this we were technically reducing our assets, but in reality if the venture failed we would not be noticeably worse off.

We were looking round the corner of the granary where all the bits and pieces 'put by' were crammed in together. There was an old fridge, tarpaulins, dustbins, park railings, electric fencing, stakes, batteries, tyres. Hardly what you could call liquid assets. Then we spotted just the thing—our almost new two-cow milking-machine.

Tom had bought it two years before at an auction sale he attended with Don Parker, a cheerfully indomitable young man who farmed everything from cows and bullocks to sheep and poultry, and grew everything from wheat and potatoes to hay and damsons, on an estate that extended to all of fifty acres. Don's wife and I always dreaded these expeditions. The two men seemed to egg each other on to buy things they did not need. They would arrive home flushed with enthusiasm over their bargains, to be greeted by cries of "What's that for?" or "We don't need that." On this occasion Tom arrived back with a milking-machine for extracting milk from two cows simultaneously.

"It'll take all the labour out of milking Angel" he explained. Angel was our capricious but much-loved house cow. "Just hook up, switch on and stand back. No more stripping away at those tiny teats of hers."

I was not impressed. Three years of milking Angel by hand, morning and night, certainly made the idea of doing the job by machine sound attractive. But I knew that by the time the machine was used, and then taken down and all the bits and pieces carted into the kitchen and washed and sterilised, the task would take twice as long as hand milking. Tom defended his purchase. "This machine is almost new and cost a fraction of the list price. They're £350 new, you know. The motor alone is worth twice what I paid for it. It'll make some money if we want to sell it. The trouble with women is you always want to do a job the hard way. You'd cut the lawn with nail scissors if you had the chance."

Living in the country I had discovered that the most fundamental difference between men and women, whatever the Equal Opportunities Commission maintains, is their attitude to machinery. Tom, like most men, believes there is a power tool for every job. I still have vivid memories of the unseasonable blizzard created in the larder when Tom insisted that my method of removing the crust of limewash on the walls with water and a scraper was ridiculously laborious. The limewash had set over the years into a covering as thick as icing on a wedding cake. He plugged in his electric drill with wire brush attachment and got to work. It did not remove much of the lime, but it certainly spread it around. Within a few minutes we looked like a couple of Father Christmases with white bushy eyebrows and thick white hair.

My method of removing the couch grass from the kitchen garden by forking up the roots and shaking them up by hand also came in for criticism. George Bolt was called in to plough the plot and Tom promised to clear it with a motorised rotovator the following spring. All might have been well had we had a normal spring. But in the spring the ground was too wet, too rough and too full of the spaghetti-like roots of the couch grass for the rotovator to function. In the end they would yield to nothing but my fork. And yes, I would love an electric motor-mower instead of the loud, shaking monster that roars up and down spitting grass in all directions—when it is working. Basically I am frightened of machines. I do not understand them, nor do I want to.

After Tom bought the milking-machine he decided we should have a second cow to go with it. We could use her milk to feed calves. A few years ago that would have been done, most economically, by buying skimmed milk from a butter factory. But such are the extraordinary mechanics of the Common Market that, in an effort to keep the price of butter down to a level that some people, at least, could afford, the price of the by-product in the process—skim milk—is kept up to a ludicrously high level. It is now so expensive that small farms like Deerpark find it cheaper to produce milk from a cow to feed the calves, rather than to buy skim milk powder for bucket-feeding.

For our extra cow we decided on an Ayrshire because they were cheaper and more amenable than Friesians. Tom went off to another sale to see what he could find.

The lorry came jolting up the drive at about four o'clock. It was a cold evening in early winter, one of those when the mists rise from the ground chilling first your feet, then your knees and then your whole body. Tom jumped down from the lorry cab.

"I've bought a super heifer. A first calver. Hell, we were lucky to get her, the price of cows is going mad. I was tempted to buy two—we'll never be able to afford to buy one again. Don bought the best of the bunch—an eight-galloner."

We let down the ramp at the back of the lorry and Mavis, as the heifer was called, came crashing out and galloped across the yard in high dudgeon. She stopped suddenly, turned and faced us; we prepared to take a flying leap over the nearest stable door. But she decided not to charge us, and with a snort and toss of her head stalked into the cow shed. This display of temper should have warned us. Tom went off to find the milking-machine. He then chained Mavis up by the simple expedient of putting some corn in the manger next to the chain. The next step was slightly more complicated. We—or rather Tom, I was keeping well clear—had to get the clusters (the suction tubes) on to her teats. For a start it was difficult to get near her. She was straining on the cow chain, sometimes going down on her knees and slashing the air angrily with her tail. Then she got to her feet, urinated, caught her tail in the stream and caught Tom a stinging swipe across the face. I had once thought the term 'you cow' as a term of abuse for humans a little unfair to our productive bovines. Not any more.

It was some years since Tom had last used a milking-machine and I soon realised that for anyone who was not adept at handling the clusters you needed two pairs of hands. Tom would get two of the tubes on, but while he was putting on the remaining two the first pair would fall off. Mad Mavis, as we quickly called her, was not helping either, moving and swaying and stamping. At last all the clusters were in place. Tom switched on the machines and prepared to stand back while it did its job. But Mavis showed herself within seconds to be ably proficient at freeing herself from the machine. I had a feeling she had played this game many times before. She turned her head, swivelled an evil eye at us and then, like Houdini, gave one shake and the clusters were off.

It took Tom about an hour to get Mavis successfully hooked up. But she had one more trick to play. When the machine was switched on there was no milk. We tried the machine on Angel and it worked perfectly. Back to Mad Mavis. Tom felt her udder. It was as tough and unyielding as a tree fungus. Mavis was sulking and was not going to relax her muscles and let her milk flow freely. Tom tried hand milking. Mad Mavis knew how to handle this situation too. She had an accurate cow kick that in one movement knocked the milker from the stool and then planted a leg firmly in the bucket. All the time her damp tail slashed the air. Eventually Tom managed to squeeze about a gallon of milk out of her and we went into the kitchen for a very late supper.

After two days of this bedlam Tom and I decided to call it a day. Luckily for us a friend of Tom's, a dog dealer from Wales, arrived at Deerpark to buy one of our collies. He looked round our stock and particularly admired Mad Mavis. "What a fine young heifer."

Tom was less enthusiastic. "Well, to tell you the truth I'm not altogether happy with her. She's a bit of a handful."

"Never did mind a cow that's a bit of bother. How much do you want for her?"

Tom named a figure, there was some haggling, then a handslap on the sale. We could not get the buyer into the house quickly enough to write the cheque, and were thankful when Mavis showed herself remarkably willing to be ushered into the dealer's lorry.

No sooner had the cow and her new owner disappeared down the farm drive than Don Parker arrived at the back door. He accepted a cup of coffee whilst Tom and I tried to guess the reason for his visit. Farmers in Micklebury did not trail up our long drive without a particular reason. It was not long before we realised his cow was being a bit of bother too.

"How's that milking-machine working?" he enquired solicitously.

"Great," replied Tom. "It really takes the work out of milking."

"Mm. How many are you doing. Only two. Mm, you could do with a couple more cows then. You're wasting your time setting the machine up to milk just two cows."

The hint that we should make an offer for a third cow hung like a cartoon bubble in the fug of the warm kitchen.

"No," explained Tom. "I don't think I'm cut out to be a cowman. I've sold the Ayrshire. Man came along yesterday and bid me for her. She's gone. Went down the road an hour ago."

A strong wave of disbelief washed over Don's face. People just did not sell cows like that. Were we pulling his leg?

"How's your cow?" asked Tom.

"Phew. Never seen an Ayrshire like her. Eight gallons a day she's giving. She's got a bag on her like a balloon. I wish the other ten cows I've got were like her."

We talked of other things but after about half an hour the conversation veered back to the magnetic subject of cows and money.

"That man who bought your cow," asked Don. "Could he do with any more? I might sell my Ayrshire if he's desperate. Mind, I wouldn't take a penny less than £20 on top of what I paid for her."

"I'll give him a ring tonight." promised Tom.

But the dog dealer was not too keen on the idea of another Ayrshire. Perhaps Mavis had already shown her true form.

Two weeks later we dropped into the Parkers for tea. An amazing sight met out eyes. There was milk everywhere. On the window-sill, on top of the freezer, and in every available space there was jugs and jugs of the stuff. There was milk in pudding basins, flower-vases, buckets, in every container the Parkers possessed.

"What's this?" asked Tom. "Setting up in competition with United Dairies?"

Mrs. Parker's face flushed with annoyance. Her lips tightened.

"Don's decided we should make some farmhouse butter."

Don came through the door at that point. "I've done the jobs, love," he said to his wife, "but you'll have to give me a hand to rope that cow."

"What cow's that?" asked Tom casually. "The one you bought at that sale?"

"Yes. Good cow but a bit frisky when you milk her. We haven't been able to get her to take to calves so we milk her out, skim off the cream and then bucket feed the calves."

"She's a really lovely cow," defended Mrs. Parker. "It's so nice to have some real creamy milk instead of that watery Friesian stuff."

The Parkers being true people of the Marches did not give up with their cow as we feeble newcomers had done. They persevered, skimming the milk to make farmhouse butter, until in time the cow settled down and accepted her role as foster mother to four calves.

All this had been a year ago. Now the only souvenir of the episode, the milking-machine, lay unused in the barn. It seemed the ideal item to sell to finance our start in the business. We advertised it in a farming magazine and, to my surprise, soon had several telephone calls about it.

"My husband won't let it go for less than £100," I told the callers with more confidence than I felt. "The motor alone is worth that." To my even greater surprise the price was agreed. The sale went ahead without a hitch. When the buyer had left with the machine, Tom and I had a cup of coffee in the kitchen. I looked at the newly-signed cheque. We were both feeling strangely cheerful. The sour incident of the Ayrshire cow and the milking-machine had turned out to our advantage after all. I had the feeling our luck was about to change.

"Things are going to go for us now," I told Tom confidently.

About a year later we met the man who had bought the milking machine.

"How's it going?" enquired Tom.

"Er, fine. Yes, fine," he added more positively. But before he collected his wits I saw a look I recognised flit through his eyes. It was an expression of the sad disillusion of a man who realises that not everything is done best by machine.

Yet for us the two-cow milker had proved a good buy—and an even better sale. For it had provided the necessary margin of capital with which to launch ourselves into the holiday trade.

# Open house

I first realised that I was pregnant when I bent down to pick up an armful of bricks from the hardcore heap outside the farmyard gate. Road-making was a regular spring task at Deerpark and that year there seemed to be more potholes than smooth patches in its surface. Our road-making techniques were not up to McAlpine's standards but they made a serviceable and inexpensive job of our farm track. First we filled the holes with bricks and stones and then we surfaced the lot with a thin topping of gravel. I was engaged in transferring to the trailer the constituents of the wall which used to stand between the living room and the dairy when a sharp attack of heart-burn made me drop the bricks and straighten up. Normally I had a cast iron stomach and I knew the cause of the pain instinctively. Tom and I had wanted another baby, but not that year, certainly not that year. The faint trilling of the telephone interrupted my thoughts and I hared round the corner into the house to answer it. It was a booking for a family of six.

"Yes, of course." I tried to suppress my panting. Breathlessness was likely to make potential guests feel uneasy. "We can offer you two double-bedded rooms and one twin-bedded room. It's a ten per cent deposit."

I wrote down the names. Poor Tom was going to be spending several weeks in our old caravan and I made a mental note to get an extra bed from somewhere. It was an encouraging further booking, before even our first guests had arrived. Then I was gripped by a cold sensation of fear. What if I was having a baby? How on earth would I manage? I had been totally swamped by fatigue with my first baby. Could I manage to cook all those fried farm-house breakfasts? Even worse, what would happen to our paying-guest enterprise if something went wrong and I was ordered to rest?

I went to find Tom. He was fiddling with the car-burettor of the garden Rotovator which had been in dry dock in the toolshed for the past year. I made my announcement.

"Just to complete the picture of our present strained circumstances I think I'm going to have a baby in December. We won't know for sure for at least a month. But I *am* sure."

Tom stopped messing about with the machine and looked up.

"That's not too terrible. When would it be? December? Well the guests will have gone by then, won't they? You didn't have any trouble last time and if the worst comes to the worst we'll just have to put people off. You city people take these things far too seriously. When I was a boy the gypsies . . ."

"I know, I know," I interrupted. I had heard this particular piece of folklore before. "The gypsies had their babies in the fields and were hop picking again after half an hour with the babies on their backs. Bully for them."

"Besides, I rather like the idea of another boy. You're not getting any younger," added Tom thoughtfully.

I had thought our predicament could not get any worse. Now I faced a whole summer of cooking, cleaning and washing while I grew into an elephant. I swore loudly and went back to the pile of bricks.

On the evening before our first guests were due to arrive Tom and I drove down the track to put up some signposts marking the way to the farm. The road was in the smoothest state it had been for years and I hoped the guests would appreciate that. As Tom hammered in the stakes to carry the signs I pondered on how our life was about to change drastically. We were about to sell our most precious possession—our way of life, our privacy, the remoteness, the peace. How jealously we had guarded that remoteness. There was no sign, no hint that the narrow wooded lane striking out by the car park of the Fox and Pheasant led to anything more than a few fields and perhaps an old barn. Beyond the end of the lane we lived in a world of our own. From our house there was no sign of any other dwelling, only the sweep of the fields, the trees and the faint far outline of the Malverns, until the foresters' massacre of the woodland revealed at night the distant lights of Leominster.

Our remoteness protected us from nosey government officials, travelling salesmen, itinerants, vandals, escaped convicts and the like. There had been times, it is true, when our isolation proved inconvenient. When friends or clients for our horses wanted to visit us they often went astray. However detailed the instructions we issued to the people we really did want to see, they would often spend hours motoring around the Herefordshire countryside. There were occasions, too, in the summer when we would arrive at the bottom of the lane, bone weary, with a couple of loads of straw behind the tractors only to find the way was blocked by a car belonging to a drinker in the nearby pub who assumed the road was unused, and was a handy adjunct to the car park.

Now we were deliberately channelling people towards

us with signs and maps and I feared that one element in our life would disappear for ever. At least Doreen had made a good job of painting the signs. Her spelling had been a slight problem and I noticed that DEADSLOW was still one word despite my correcion of the pencilled outline. Tom hammered a large headed nail in the middle. We had had a similar problem with the sign for the farmyard reading CARS PARKED AT OWNERS RISK. Doreen could not believe that the apostrophe went after the S, and so omitted it altogether.

As I sat on the bank watching Tom fix the signs I wondered how it would all turn out. Would we even yet have to sell up because we could not make such a small farm pay? Or would the farm holidays be our salvation? After all, Conrad Hilton had started by taking lodgers in his father's house. If I were honest I would have to admit that I loathed entertaining. I could never successfully combine the cooking with the talking. Conversation always took an interesting turn just as I had disappeared into the kitchen. And at Deerpark such entertaining as we had been able to do had meant trying—and usually failing—to fit all the shopping and cooking around a full day's farm work outside. Would my cooking pass muster, I wondered? Try as I might my pastry was still horrible, so I would have to cheat and use the frozen stuff. Should we tell them about all the house's little quirks like the sitting-room door that needed a shoulder against it because it tended to stick, or the lavatory seat that had a castrating effect because it would not stay up however we adjusted it? No, perhaps not. It was better to show people around with an air of confidence as if we had been doing it for years. Let them discover the farm's idiosyncrasies for themselves.

The house was all ready for its new role. It had never been cleaner. I had been up at five o'clock one morning and had painted the main bedroom ceiling before

Anthony had a chance to 'help'. In the living room was a card declaring that coffee was 12p a cup, tea was 10p a pot. The window-sill was covered with brochures tempting people to visit the many castles, museums, historic houses and gardens in the area. A good supply of brochures was important because the town's tourist office, a table in the local library, was closed on Sundays and Mondays—which were the first two days of most people's holidays. The extra furniture had not arrived, but the removers promised faithfully it was on the way. Meanwhile the permanent residents of Deerpark would have to manage with the bathroom stool and the telephone stool to sit on at meal times, as the guests had two of the kitchen chairs.

The weather too was beginning to look more promising. Slowly, almost imperceptibly, spring was creeping up on us. I had heard a cuckoo at long last, and many other birds had begun to flock back to our pastures. Our favourite summer visitors, the swallows, were returning to their old nests in the eaves of the house and in the gutterings round the barns. I never felt life was complete at Deerpark until the air was dotted with these graceful birds soaring and diving around the farmyard. Other birds too that had gone missing during the long wet winter months were flying in for the summer. Wagtails did their stationary bobbing act on the garden fence. Sparrows bathed, twirled and preened themselves in the water in the potholes in the drive. Cheeky chaffinches hopped onto the kitchen window-sill, and bluetits hung like miniature gymnasts on the japonica that was covering the southern wall of the house with tiny red rosettes.

Up at the dewpond I had seen a pair of wild ducks taking a tour of inspection, poking about with a slightly superior and supercilious expression that I was to come to know only too well on the faces of people 'off the road' who came to inspect the bedrooms. But best of all, several herons had taken to feeding by the pond. We would creep up on them and watch them dipping their beaks slightly disdainfully into the muddy waters. When they spotted us they would rise into the air beating their great wings and drift off effortlessly to their next port of call.

We had a clear view of the birdlife around the farm because the late spring meant little foliage on the trees. A few of the shrubs in the hedgerows were coming reluctantly into leaf, but as I looked about me the great thick woods of oak and ash were still bare and black. At night the temperature still dropped sharply and the ground was gripped by iron-hard frosts that inhibited the growth of grass. The weather had been too cold for us to turn out the cattle from their winter quarters in the barns. We could put them out by day, but at night were still letting them back inside for some corn and some warmth. Their nightly rushing and cavorting would make an unusual cabaret for the guests to watch while they were eating their evening meal.

Tom finished planting the signs and we drove back up the track. The car still bounced up and down despite all the work and stone we had put into the road. We stopped on the rise by the dewpond and I left the car to open the gate. This was the spot from which people would have their first glimpse of the farm, a glimpse that came just when they were giving up hope of finding Deerpark. I caught my breath. The house rose up out of the curving green pastures, a house in the middle of nowhere, a house in its own world. On both sides stone farm buildings folded round it protectively while huge spreading oaks stood guard. The golden rays of the bright evening sun slanted down through the screen of trees to the west giving the pinkish sandstone of the house a warm glow. More oak trees dotted the pasture at the side of the house.

On their branches the bright sunlight picked up the furry, fat buds about to burst into leaf at long last.

Tom got out of the car and joined me: "Deerpark might have its drawbacks, but they certainly can't complain about the look of the place."

Our first guests, a middle-aged couple called Price, arrived after lunch the following day. Tom and I both went out to meet them and show them where to park the car. We were taken aback to see they were both ashen-faced with fear after their trip up the drive and with apprehension about what was to follow. This was a situation we had to become accustomed to handling. Most people were worn out before they started their holiday (that was why they needed a break), they had had a long car journey through weekend traffic and then to cap it all, they had to cope with our roadway. We soon learnt that it was very important to offset this by a truly warm welcome.

Tom took the Prices' luggage and we ushered them into the house for a complimentary cup of tea. They soon recovered and set out to explore the farm. Our guest house was launched.

At first it seemed odd to be playing host to complete strangers, people who ate the best food, on the best crockery, using the best cutlery and who watched our colour television in the comfort of our living room while we slummed it in the kitchen. In those early days I found that cooking the evening meal was like tackling a dinner party every day of the week. But before long it became no more trouble than cooking lunch for my own brood. I did however have to learn a fine sense of timing to interweave serving at table in the sitting room with cooking in the kitchen. I had to resist the temptation to throw the soup on the table and rush back to the kitchen to rescue the chops under the grill. It was important, I found, to the guests' peace of mind to always appear to have everything easily under control. The rest of the household also had some lessons to learn. One of the first was to ensure that Tom and Doreen did not appear on the breakfast-time scene at nine o'clock on the dot, and use for their own drinks the kettleful of water I had ready for the guests' tea or coffee.

I was pleasantly surprised when, on the first morning of the Prices' visit, I discovered Mrs. Price had made their bed. Other farmers' wives who took visitors told me this was normal. Indeed they complained loudly when people did not. The Prices, like almost all our guests, also left the bathroom spotless. We appreciated these small gestures enormously. Not only was any extra help a godsend; dirty guests made us feel our home was not our own, but occupied territory.

I fairly quickly got the measure of the work involved in taking guests, and learnt to cope with it. Only the washing up remained an enormous chore. On farms in any event there seems to be an invisible force in the kitchen remorselessly creating piles of dirty crockery by the sink. Now I found that, in the evening in particular, every available surface in the scullery was covered with stacks of dirty dishes all waiting to be washed before I could set about finishing my share of chores in the farm-yard, and bath Anthony and put him to bed. Then I cooked supper for Tom, Doreen and myself and washed that up before staggering upstairs and collapsing into bed.

We solved the problem of getting a bath ourselves either by having a good soak in the middle of the day, or sometimes in the middle of the night. The guests always seemed to be in the bathroom when it was time for Anthony's bath, so I used the kitchen sink for him. He adored the change and took to climbing into the sink fully clothed when it was full of water during the day.

It was lucky for us that our first guests were people like the Prices. If we had started with some of the horrors who subsequently stayed at Deerpark I do not think we would have had the heart to carry on. But the Prices were one of the friendliest couples ever to stay with us. They loved the farm and everything about it. Tom and I found, too, that we enjoyed their company. Indeed it was a long time since we had had the chance to talk fully to anyone from 'outside'. Even the weather favoured them. There was sunshine for six days out of their seven, and the Prices watched the television forecast with grim satisfaction as the announcer daily drew a line over an area that included their home county and filled it with magnetic clouds releasing raindrops. They left on the Saturday bearing two dozen of our eggs as souvenirs and promising they would be back the following May.

We then had a break for several weeks. It took me time to learn that if you want a continuous stream of out-of-season visitors you must advertise continuously. But in any event we could not have taken in many people, because the extra furniture had still not appeared. And the weather had again taken a turn for the worse.

We turned the cattle out for good only on the day the Prices left. Even so, the cattle did not relish their freedom. They stood cold and disconsolate outside the farmyard gate waiting in vain to be let into the warm barn, waiting for the weather to change, waiting for summer. As they churned up the roadway outside the house and top dressed it with mushy manure we waited with them, but without their inexhaustible bovine patience. At times I wondered if it would ever stop raining or whether our next lot of guests would face not only the bumpy drive but a smelly quagmire under foot when they reached the farmyard gate. Doreen kept saying: "Hell, you pommie bastards, where's your English summer? Our winters in Queensland are warmer than this." Why is it that overseas visitors seem to think the British are personally responsible for their weather? The apparent bygone omnipotence of the colonial administrators, I suppose.

Then summer exploded on the countryside. In the long sunlit days the grass grew lavishly. Overnight the fields seemed to dry up and burst into flower. Sodden fields, bare trees and grey, tired sky disappeared. Thick grass brushed our legs as we strode across the fields, warm sunshine browned our faces and arms. And there was blossom everywhere. By the house the chestnut trees were bowed down with red and white candles, in the garden of the Fox and Pheasant the lilacs emitted the sweet scent of summer, and through the foliage of the roadside hedgerow the cider orchards were pink clouds of blossom.

When the temperature reached the seventies I grabbed my bathing costume and set off for a swim in the dew-pond. When I got there I could hardly believe my eyes. The previous day the pool had been deep enough for a determined bather; now it was half-empty, with hardly enough water for a decent paddle. It must have sprung a leak somewhere. I wondered if this was anything to do with the fact that during the drought the pool had dried up and we had taken the opportunity to get the local contractors to bulldoze out its deep layers of sediment. I rushed off to find Tom.

"I'm sure we've ruined it," I moaned. "Those dew-ponds are constructed in a very special way. The method is thousands of years old. They lined them with straw and then compacted the mud on top by running cattle through them. I'm sure you're not supposed to attack them with bulldozers."

"Nonsense, woman," yelled Tom. "Look here, it's running down this hole."

"Hole? Hole?" I was incredulous. But sure enough Tom had found the leak. The water was pouring down a hole like water down the plughole of a bath. And it was a very long hole indeed. When the pool was enlarged we had found some old, disused drainpipes set into one side of it. They had appeared broken and blocked with mud so we never thought of disturbing them. Now those old pipes were draining the water out of the pond.

"And I can tell you where it's going." We turned to see the figure of our neighbour to the north, John Hopkins, looming up. "It's all in my sugar-beet field. I've just come up to see where it's all coming from." John's sugar-beet field was at least half a mile away.

"Those drains were laid by Napoleonic prisoners of war," he explained. "They put them in at least three feet deep and all the digging was done by hand. We came across some on my farm that were down six feet. And we think *we* work hard." He paused and laughed.

"Round here everyone thinks they've got dewponds and springs and other mysterious and wonderful sources of water, but I think it's all due to those old drains. They break up and then the water hangs about forming a hollow. Over the years people enlarge them and more water collects." John's explanations were sometimes so utterly bizarre that we were inclined to accept them for their sheer ingenuity.

We blocked the outlet of the drain with concrete, and the water level in the pool stopped dropping. Later on in the summer John had the best crop of sugar beet seen in the county for decades. Coincidence perhaps, or good management, but there is just an outside chance that half a pondful of dew had something to do with it.

Summer had definitely arrived at Deerpark but not the extra furniture for our visitors. After a dozen phone calls I dicovered it was languishing in a warehouse in Harlesden. An apologetic voice at the end of the telephone said: "We'll definitely get it to you in ten days' time.

It's the Bank Holiday, you know. We can't get it to you before that."

I had visions of the non-paying members of the Deerpark community spending a week without chairs to sit on at mealtimes and without blankets on their beds.

"I know it's the Bank Holiday," I said evenly, trying to keep my temper. "That is why I need my furniture. I need it for my guest house—the season opens this weekend. What am I supposed to do? Rush out and buy a load of blankets and chairs?"

It was another example of the 'Law of Diminishing Responsibility.' This law of business practice states: 'The larger the company the less responsibility it takes for its mistakes.' That year the Post Office had omitted Tom's name from the telephone directory, a mistake that cost us about two hundred pounds in lost business with our horses. They were pleasantly apologetic, but that did not bring us back our two hundred pounds. But these mistakes happen on a smaller scale every day of our working lives. The assistant in the ironmongers for instance, gives you half-inch screws instead of the three-quarter ones you ordered. Of course they change them, but the time that takes up and the petrol the car uses to make the return journey are yours.

The firm of removers that had been shunting my furniture around the country for the past six weeks had been paid in advance, so it was no loss to them to hang on to it for another ten days. Rudeness never pays, so I decided to beg. That brought about a softening of attitude and a compromise was reached—at our cost, of course. They would get the furniture to Hereford by the end of the week. We would collect it from there in our stock lorry.

That we did, and by the weekend the house was not only spotless again, but it also had its full complement of chairs, blankets, crockery and chests of drawers. Once again it was Saturday lunchtime and we were waiting slightly apprehensively for our next batch of visitors, a family of five called the Thorntons.

We went out to greet them as their blue Marina drew up at the farmyard gate. Introductions were made and Mr. Thornton smiled slightly patronisingly. "The last farm we stayed at was rather like this. It was in the Pyrenees and all the cows had bells round their necks." The Thornton children burst out of the car like cops in a crime serial and rushed off to pet the collies: a boy and a girl of about ten or eleven and a real demon of a little boy aged four, already highly-skilled at tormenting his elders. He often wore a towelling sweater with a peaked hood so we soon nicknamed him 'Hobgoblin Thornton'.

It turned out to be one of the most harrowing weeks I was to experience over a couple of seasons of taking paying guests. Doreen was away and Tom's hands were full with two horses to be broken in. Within a couple of days all the Thorntons had developed honking colds. "We always get the sniffles on us when we go on holiday," laughed Mrs. Thornton. Anthony and I caught it too and as I stood at the sink in the evening tackling the ever-mounting pile of washing up, my bones aching, my head splitting, my nose running and my son clinging to my leg and grisling with the same complaints, I thought I was earning every penny the Thorntons were paying.

The Thorntons' day—and mine while they were at Deerpark—started at five o'clock in the morning when the two elder children kicked off with a game of tag in the upstairs passage. Tom was spared this rude awakening as the Thornton parents had our room. I was sleeping in the spare bed in Anthony's room, but Tom was sleeping in the sanctuary of the caravan, set well away in Bay One of the Dutch barn. After a couple of days and several reprimands from their parents the elder children tempered their enthusiasm slightly and postponed their early morning games until six o'clock. A screaming and shouting session in the farmyard was followed by breakfast where Hobgoblin Thornton showed his paces. Dropping his fresh orange juice on the carpet and weeping noisily for a second glass was a typical start. At both breakfast and supper he would look at his plate, wrinkle his nose and grizzle: "I don't like bacon/sausages/tomatoes/roast beef/chicken/chops." Sometimes he would make a mistake and I'd say:

"That's lucky, because this is lamb."

After the breakfast there was a session of what I called 'wrecking the joint', with all three children hurtling about the rooms, the corridors and the garden. But the Thorntons were not really exceptionally destructive or noisy; they were just high-spirited because they were on holiday. The basic trouble was that Deerpark was a farmhouse, not a hotel. It was not built for two families living on top of each other, nor decorated and furnished with tough, indestructible products. A few over-enthusiastic tugs, for instance, soon brought the curtain rails down. Mr. Thornton was apologetic:

"I'll fix them for you. You don't mind my asking do you, but who put them up originally?"

I admitted that the curtain rails were my handiwork.

"I thought I saw a woman's touch there," said Mr. Thornton triumphantly. "No rawlplugs."

Tom and I took all this in good heart. It was the electric kettle that irked me most. As Mrs. Thornton carried it into the house she remarked casually: "For our thermoses, so we won't have to bother you."

But it was not only for their thermoses. It was soon clear that they were brewing up in the bedroom. There were tea and coffee stains on the carpet and ring marks from mugs on the furniture. I know the English on holiday have a long tradition of brewing up cuppas in their hotel bedrooms, but I was annoyed, perhaps unreasonably, that people were doing it in my home, because they were too tight-fisted to pay me 10p for a pot of tea.

We swallowed hard and realised these were only minor irritants. At least none of the children had tried to set fire to the house or caused any serious damage. It was to be over a year before we had our first pyromaniac.

# Jubilee spots

The Jubilee festivities came as a break in our apprenticeship to the holiday trade. Jubilee day in Micklebury was celebrated with all the patriotic exuberance that characterises small rural communities on high days and holidays, and which makes them places to live in rather than merely to exist in. In common with other villages throughout the length and breadth of the British Isles, no such day of national celebration is complete without an acrimonious and sustained row that splits the whole community. On this occasion most of the disputes seemed to centre on what should be done with the money which was raised through coffee evenings, bazaars and raffles. Many villages had one faction which wanted the bulk of the money donated to the Queen's Jubilee Fund, and another that wanted it spent on a beanfeast for themselves.

In Micklebury there was at first a consensus of opinion. Almost everyone agreed it was right and proper that most of the money should go on Jubilee celebrations in the village itself.

The weather was less ecstatic. Jubilee day dawned wan and miserable and there was every sign the day would be literally, if not figuratively, a washout. The grey, weary sky chucked fistfuls of rain into a chilling north-west wind. It was certainly not the kind of day for standing on an exposed lawn and chatting to your neighbours. But by lunchtime the rain had moved on to ruin someone else's day and the sun appeared from time to time between the billowing cumulus.

Micklebury's Jubilee celebrations started with a grand parade of fancy dress contestants from the car park of the Fox and Pheasant to the spacious ground of the house of the village squire, Mr. Hanson. I say squire, but that is not an exact description of Mr. Hanson's position in the social hierarchy of Micklebury. The village had neither manor house, nor squire, just as it no longer had a policeman, doctor, postmaster or blacksmith. It could get by without the last four, but there were occasions when a chieftain was needed. Mr. Hanson, as the largest landowner in the area, stepped in to fill the gap.

Leading the parade in fine style was Mr. Hanson's son, Rodney, in a highwayman's menacing black mask and black cloak, astride his twenty-year-old grey hunter mare, a docile lady called Amanda. One of Micklebury's claims to fame was the legend that a notorious highwayman had taken refuge in the Hansons' house after an unsuccessful attempt to relieve some of the local gentry of their possessions or their lives. His horse, exhausted by the chase, collapsed outside the stables and died. They buried her there, and a plaque now marks the spot where 'the faithful mare breathed her last'. In keeping with the legend and with the historic occasion Rodney Hanson's mare provided the best entertainment of the afternoon by suddenly going berserk among the motley collection of Bo-peeps, Britannias, lions and unicorns.

When we reached the Hansons' lawn we all stood to attention while God Save the Queen crackled faintly over the public address system and the celebrations were declared open by the chairman of the parish council. Prizes were distributed for the fancy dress parade and then most of the afternoon was filled with children's sports and the presentation of Jubilee mugs to every child in the village. Anthony clutched his mug possessively and was totally confused by the festivities. Finally there was the high spot of the afternoon—the Jubilee tea. Tom and I thankfully enjoyed this half-day off from the farm. We seldom had the chance to get away even for a couple of hours, because it was difficult to find someone willing to babysit in such a remote place—even if we were not up to our elbows in work. Village occasions to which we could take Anthony were therefore the only opportunities we had to take a break. I especially appreciated a meal, even sandwiches and cakes, that I had not had to cook myself. For now every meal that I ate was preceded by cooking two meals—one for ourselves and one for the guests.

Yet not everyone in the village was happy with the tea. Some of the older farmers complained that the organisers had perpetrated a heinous crime. In Herefordshire of all places the sandwiches were filled with Argentinian spam. Joady, a solid slow-moving smallholder who seemed to adopt the role of village seer, was the leader of the protest movement. He snorted in disgust: "We don't eat tinned-meat sandwiches in Micklebury. Everyone ud ate those sandwiches has come out in a rash. Jubilee spots I call um."

There was a tidy sum of money still in the Jubilee kitty and Joady canvassed support amongst the villagers for a Jubilee supper to eradicate the shameful memory of the Jubilee tea. For a man who had lived most of his life on Wye salmon and salt bacon, he reckoned his priorities were the right ones. He wanted a supper with "Cold beef, pickles, bread and butter and cider." As he rode around the country lanes on his old tractor canvassing support for his cause he was hailed everywhere as the 'Spam King'.

He visited us personally at Deerpark. "This is a farming

area. We produce good meat. If I laid out a dinner like that for a team of shearers I'd be catching, shearing and winding all by myself all afternoon."

To decide the fate of the remaining Jubilee money a public meeting was held in the village hall. Under a delightful frieze of squirrels and birds which had been put together from dried leaves by the local primary school children, about fifty of the inhabitants of Micklebury overflowed on flimsy stacking chairs, their jaws clenched and their eyes glinting with the fervour of people with a mission.

But they were not intent on the same mission. Ideas ranged from planting commemorative cherry trees, creating a garden around the village hall, giving a tea for pensioners, with presentations of commemorative ash-trays, to a donation to the restoration fund for the church bells. Joady was adamant:

"That money was collected for a binge. It should be spent on a binge." Somewhat to the surprise of the committee the majority of the people in the hall agreed with him and Joady's Jubilee supper won the day. The old man was jubilant and told a circle of supporters afterwards. "They thought I be simple. They shouted me down at the first meeting. Wouldn't even let me say my piece. I had my heavy artillery behind me this time. My friends."

We thought that would be the end of the altercation. The Jubilee supper took place three weeks later. We could not get to it, but report had it that the beef was excellent and the cider copious. But not all Joady's opponents accepted the defeat with good grace. The incident split the village down the middle. Several people boycotted the Jubilee supper and it was many months before the incident faded into Micklebury folklore.

A good, lusty argument over what may to an outsider seem a minor issue, which in due course becomes an apparent matter of principle, is all part of village life. For farmers it is one way of enjoying some light relief from the life and death struggle to make a living from the land. A good argument, the bruises of which soon fade, makes a change.

From Jubilee day onwards the holiday season gathered pace and the weeks in my reservations' diary were now filling up rapidly. We restricted our numbers to a single family, or a family and friends, because of the pressure on our single bathroom—which was also our single lavatory. Most of the time we took in only couples, a policy which I was thankful we had adopted, as I was already beginning to suffer from the pervasive fatigue which had been a feature of my first pregnancy.

The weather was not being very helpful, either for holiday-making or for the haymaking, which was the next major event due on our farming calendar. Cement-coloured skies exuded day after day a continuous cold drizzle. Yet I no longer loathed wet weather. The memory of the previous year's drought was too sharp for that. In the interludes between the rain storms the re-freshed world seemed closer to us. The days of drought had seemed to put life at arm's length. Perhaps this had been an optical illusion, created by the heat shimmering on rock-hard ground. But it was more than that. Swallows had soared high in the sky like tiny toy kites, and even the moles had disappeared underground, pursuing the earthworms which had burrowed ever deeper in search of moisture.

When the skies darken over our plateau the world moves in closer. On the northern horizon the sweep of Clee Hill, half a county away, can look barely a mile distant when rain is in the air. From the ridge by the dewpond we can see the Norman tower of the priory church rising above the house roofs, so clear that we can almost see people in the streets. Once the rain begins the swallows splash in the water in the potholes, dunking their heads and ruffling their wings with gay exuberance.

In the evenings arcs of pure colour swept across the sky, rainbows that looked so solid it was tempting to rush out and see if there was, indeed, a legendary crock of gold buried where the end seemed to pierce the ground by the dewpond.

Our first arrivals after the Jubilee seemed, however, to have some influence with higher authorities. The Watsons were a charming, elderly couple and Mr. Watson announced with complete confidence that he always brought the good weather with him on his travels. As a young man he had helped on a farm in Devon at hay-making time. So invariably did his arrival there coincide with a fine spell that the farmer would wait for him before cutting his hay. We looked at Mr. Watson dis-believingly, and smiled politely at such twaddle. But we had dismissed Mr. Watson's assertions too lightly. The next day the sky began to clear bit by bit, as if all the clouds were being vacuumed up. By the second day of the Watsons' holiday the sun had dried the sparrows' baths. Haymaking was now a real possibility. We ummed and ahed as we did every year, unable to take the momentous decision of when to start mowing. Then Tom grabbed the phone and asked Rivers, the contractor, to cut our hay the following day. When it turned out to be a day of brilliant sunshine Mr. Watson allowed himself only a small, if very confident, smile.

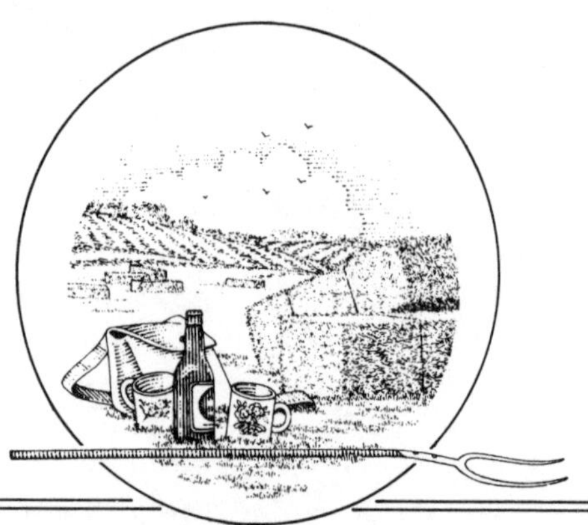

# Haymaking fever

Haymaking brought the first clash between our role as farmers and our role as guest-house proprietors. Haymaking is always a time of high tension on a small stock farm. It is the pivot on which all our agrarian fortunes turn. We must have an ample supply of well-made, nutritious hay if we are going to be able to feed our cattle economically throughout the winter. It is the one form of winter forage which we can garner from our own fields. Without it, our problems would be insurmountable. To buy in hay from other farms would be too expensive, to buy in processed feeding stuffs even more expensive.

The quality of the hay crop depends, above all else, on the weather. The great enemy of the haymaker is rain. Too much rain means that the crop—and our margin of profits for the coming year—is literally a washout. If the rain falls when the grass is ready for the mower, the harvesting will be delayed, and the quality of the resulting hay will suffer. Worse still, if rain falls once the crop is cut, much of the nutriment can be washed out of it and, at the worst, the swathes of grass can be rotted and blackened.

Fortunately these dangers from the weather are not as bad as they used to be. Technology has done much to help. More detailed long-range weather forecasts are one aid. More efficient farm machinery is another. The machinery makers have devised new, powerful hay tedders—machines to toss and turn the cut hay so as to speed up its drying. We need now only four days of consecutive sunshine to dry out a newly-cut crop to the point at which it can be baled. Even if rain does come, these new tedders greatly help the process, once fine weather returns, drying out the sodden crop by chucking the grass into the air and scattering it out for the sun and wind to get at it before it can sweat and grow mouldy.

Haymaking and harvest times were always weeks of frantic activity at Deerpark. Tom often needed a hand in the fields, as well as a regular delivery of tea and sandwiches from the kitchen. There were huge meals to cook for casual helpers. And now there were guests to cope with as well. Luckily nothing much went wrong with the Watsons' week apart from the roast chicken drying out one night. The Watsons did not mind at all. Indeed they thought I had cooked them an authentic country dish. Mr. Watson exclaimed: "That was delicious. Was it rabbit?" I had to admit in some confusion that it was not. There was further confusion later that evening when Mrs. Watson watched Anthony playing in the front garden. He had a small plastic bag over his hand which held a long, thin stick.

Mrs. Watson smiled. "What a dear little boy he is. Always so busy. What's he playing at now?"

Realisation dawned on me. The artificial insemination expert had come to inseminate Angel that morning and Anthony had watched the procedure closely.

"I don't know what he's pretending," I mumbled and backed out of the door rapidly with the empty coffee cups. My son would find the facts of life very confusing when they were explained to him.

But the haymaking dragged on for weeks. Mr. Watson's good weather departed with him at the end of the week. Thirteen days after cutting the first patch we still had not got any of the hay in. A week of wintery gales had followed the fine start. Then the weather forecast promised a fine day with some sunshine after lunch. Tom spread the hay out with the tedder to dry off the dew, and was about to collect it back into rows ready to be baled, when a huge black cloud casually rolled in from the west and released an afternoon's rain on us. Two thirds of our hay crop was lying there cut, and was now all but ruined. The grass was at the most critical stage of all. Having been once wet and subsequently dried, it was highly absorbent. A real soaking could make it disintegrate. Unless the next day was one of truly sweltering heat we were going to end up with thirteen acres of rank fuzz that would cost £30 to bale and then would have to be burnt. An expensive bonfire. There was nothing we could do but go back to the house and watch the Wimbledon women's singles finals. Advanced technology does not come up with all the answers. When nature outmanoeuvres you there is not much you can do. At least the singles finals, in which Virginia Wade carried the day, were so enthralling that we almost forgot about our unfortunate hay crop.

To our utter astonishment we woke the next morning to a blast of sunshine. Even at seven in the morning we knew it was going to be one of those days that prompt newspaper headlines of PHEW WHAT A SCORCHER! Green glossy grass shimmered under a steely blue sky; around us the countryside was bright, crisp and clean as if the world was newly created. By lunchtime the pools on the drive had dried up. After tea Tom was at long last able to start our final baling. By the next day all thirteen acres of hay were neatly stacked in tumps of six bales apiece, and the remaining five acres were lying cut into neat swathes. That second patch took a mere three days to make in the searing heat. Eighteen days after we started haymaking two thousand three hundred bales were bursting out of the Dutch barn. Not all of it was top quality, but it was good enough to feed the many mouths on the farm during the coming winter months.

I congratulated myself on not having allowed the stress of all this to become known to the guests. Indeed I was gradually learning that one of the arts of the good landlady is to know how much—or how little—to talk to the guests. I was learning, too, with some surprise how little many townspeople know about the country. Even though I was a relatively new emigrant from city streets myself, some of the questions surprised me.

"How does the milkman get up here?" they asked. Or, "What do you do about the dustbins? Whaaaat! Take the rubbish sacks down to the crossroads?"

One new arrival asked me quite reasonably: "Now, what about papers in the morning?"

"Papers? Papers?" I repeated like an idiot. I was dog tired and I did not understand what papers he was asking about.

"I'd like a copy of the *Daily Telegraph*," he continued. Morning newspapers, that was it. We received our newspaper after lunch, collecting it from a house in the village where it was left by the milkman. I had quite forgotten that for many people breakfast was not complete without a newspaper.

Many of their misconceptions were understandable.

"You milk all those, do you?" asked one elderly gentleman as a herd of forty half-grown maiden heifers galloped past the window. And the idea that a cow had to produce a calf annually to maintain her milk supply struck the vast majority of our guests as quite unnecessarily fecund.

In contrast the children who stayed at Deerpark were impressively knowledgeable. I had expected little horrors who thought that milk came out of bottles and carrots out of tins. Not a bit of it. Some of the older children even knew the difference between wheat and barley straw. And one lively seven-year-old boy remarked to me as he watched an Aberdeen Angus bullock jump on a heifer.

"That's a bullock, but he can't."

Because farm guests were seen by all the village as a valuable part of Micklebury's income, they tended to be spared, even in the bar of the Fox and Pheasant, that teasing which the countryman likes to indulge in when he comes up against the town-dweller, and particularly the very knowledgeable town-dweller.

Salesmen, especially insurance salesmen, were considered fair game not only by man-eating farm dogs, but also by leg-pulling farmers. John Hopkins sometimes speaks nostalgically of the day they evened the score with a salesman for accident insurance. This salesman visited the area every couple of years and in a hard-sell, house-to-house campaign persuaded people to buy extra insurance cover that later they often thought to be more than they needed. One day in late September John Hopkins, and another smallholder, Martin Blackwell, were helping Don Parker lay some concrete outside his pigsties. It started to rain so they rang the Ready Mixed concrete company and told them to cancel the next load and then settled down to a cup of tea. Their relaxing afternoon was interrupted by a ring at the door. Peeping out from behind the curtains—for Don thought it might be his wife who had forgotten her key—they made out a dapper figure with highly-polished hair, highly-polished shoes and highly-polished smile. The insurance man.

John Hopkins went to the door first. "You Mr. Parker?"

asked the insurance man as he took a deep breath prior to making his sales pitch.

"Nah," said John Hopkins.

Then Martin Blackwell emerged. "Are you Mr. Parker?" asked the insurance man.

"Nah." A shake of the head.

Then Don Parker wandered through the door. "Ah," said the salesman, with brisk hopefulness. "Mr. Parker?"

Don tried to stall him. "Which one?" But the sales manual obviously provided the answer to that. The salesman countered: "Which one are you?"

"The son," replied Don. With a sigh of relief the salesman launched into his scripted sales message. Don listened and was won over. After he had signed a cheque the salesman casually asked who lived at the next farm along the road.

"Oh, that's John Hopkins," replied John Hopkins. "And you want to try Martin Blackwell up the road, he could well be interested in some extra insurance. Look, they are both a bit off the beaten track. We'll draw you a map."

John Hopkins was not exaggerating. Both farms were about two miles off the road at the end of gated farm tracks—and it was raining and represented a major detour to find two men he was already speaking to.

The rain let up a little so the three men decided to go over to Eardisland and watch the gas pipeline being laid. John Hopkins smiles when he recalls his second meeting with the insurance saleman.

"When I was coming back at about five o'clock I passed the insurance salesman. You know how narrow the road is there and how you have to slow down to pass people. He recognised me and took both hands off the steering wheel and gave me a double 'V' sign. Well, you could understand him being upset. Best laugh we've had for ages."

Meanwhile my own education in the ins and outs of the holiday business was continuing—sometimes to my cost. One delightful family, the Adamses—parents and two boys in their late teens—came to stay for ten days. For a couple of days the Adamses were model guests. They liked the farm, promised to return next year and so on. Then Mr. Adams said:

"Oh, by the way, we will be leaving on Thursday next week, not staying the extra two days. That's not inconvenient, is it?"

"Of course not. That's quite all right." They were so pleasant it seemed churlish to demand two thirds of the sum for their cancelled days. And, after all, they said they would be back again.

The evening before they left Mr. Adams asked: "Would it be more convenient for you if we had an early breakfast tomorrow?"

"Yes it would," I answered.

Mr. Adams smiled. "We want to get away early but instead of asking outright I put it in a way that seemed to be for your benefit. I'm a personnel officer. We always try to put what *we* want in terms that appear to be doing the workforce a favour."

"Oh I see, that's clever." I thought back to the way they had booked the holiday and then cancelled the extra days. Reluctantly I twigged. They had never intended to stay ten days from the outset. It was a little ruse to make me accept a Wednesday to Wednesday booking. The Bakers' warning came back to me.

In the kitchen I told Tom: "With my complete and sycophantic agreement I have just been done out of a week's booking. In future I will stick to the Bakers' advice and ask people to cough up if they go home early."

Of course we never saw the Adamses again.

Yet the sting of this experience and of the countless

other problems which are part and parcel of the landlady-guest relationship was, I found, remarkably eased when I had one more cheque to put into the bank to offset the bills which came in remorselessly, and when I paused to think what other nightmarish problems would be on our doorstep had we not embarked on this venture.

By the third week of July we were well into the swing of taking guests and were preparing for the school holiday rush. Then Doreen announced she was leaving. There were family problems in Australia and she was going home. Doreen's job had been with the horses and she had not, in fact, helped much with the guests. The main qualification for running a farm guest house, I was learning, was several years experience as a housewife. You needed the same ability to do six jobs at once. But she had helped to look after Anthony at critical moments and she was there in reserve to lend a hand peeling potatoes or serving at table if my energies had reached their limit. There was no time to advertise for anyone to take her place, nor could we afford to pay a girl any more. We had the straw harvest in front of us and the selling of our cattle. Tom and I would just have to manage on our own.

# Harvest holidays

As July ended the long grey days continued. Our world was cool and dry; miserable weather for holidaymakers but perfect for beef farmers. For once the countryside seemed at peace with itself. A gentle stillness crept over the rich green fields that looked more fertile than I could ever remember. It was as if nature was determined to erase all possible memories of the drought a year ago. In the wide, sweeping valley that separated us from the Welsh mountains the aftermath of the hay crops, where the grass was cropped like a crew cut, turned the meadows and pastures into a smooth sea of greenness. It was the light, glowing green of grass untainted by ferti- lisers. Most farmers in the Marches could only afford 'to wop on the artificial' in the early spring to promote a vigorous and vital early growth of lush emerald grass. Later on in the summer nature was left to cope on her own, or perhaps with the aid of an occasional dressing of manure.

There is a special and momentous characteristic about every month in the farming calendar. The end of July is the peak of the wonderful riotous growing season. In another fortnight the countryside will begin to go to seed. Then all the corn will have ripened, occasional brown leaves will appear on the trees, like grey hairs on the head of a celebrated sex-symbol, and the pastures look suddenly sapped and tired. Cattle and sheep will munch their way through all the tender grass leaving the coarse weeds sticking up in ragged clumps; brown spears of dead docks, dusty patches of nettles, aggressive groups of purple-capped thistles. But now the cattle grazed contentedly, spread out in lines as they chomped steadily through the lush grass. No gad flies tormented them, or made them 'gad' about the pastures in a galloping frenzy with their tails stuck high in the air. No rain drove them under the huge spreading branches of the old decaying oaks. The countryside was strangely silent for the time of year; not even the whisper of a combine harvester could be heard. Our neighbours muttered: "Late crops, heavy yields."

Now that we were in the tourism business I was beginning, however, to formulate another calendar in my mind, to flank that of the farming year. For tourism the end of July marks the high season for visitors, the start of a six week frenzy of cooking, vacuuming, bed-making, linen washing, dish washing. The cooking, serving and washing up for the visitors and my own family occupied about seven hours every day; when the other chores were added in, it made a working day of about fourteen hours. Yet, rather to my surprise, I found I was enjoying this new career of head cook and bottle-washer.

The columns of the visitors' book were filling up as not only the adults but the children too entered their names punctiliously with their comments. "Nice work," remarked two energetic girls of about ten and eleven who, on a dull and uninspiring day, had removed an astonishing quantity of muck from one of the cattle pens. They were amongst our most attractive visitors, with lively imaginations as well as lively natures. As their parents' elderly Hillman slowly negotiated the farm road they stood on the running boards, one on each side, pretending to be on safari. They played badminton on the front pasture. They joined in eagerly when we had a rodeo with our Shetland pony Alice, who is devoted to small children but loathes adults. My son, Anthony, starved of company for so long, changed from being a shy, bewildered child in company, to a sociable, laughing extrovert. Towards our adult visitors he showed an almost old-fashioned courtesy. He approached all new arrivals with an air of intense concern and holding out a hand would lead them into the house. With equal serious-ness he appointed himself gatekeeper of the farmyard gate, opening and closing it for the guests' cars—a practice encouraged by frequent rewards of sweets and chocolates.

On the whole we had few difficult customers. We found that there was a major advantage in dealing with enquiries ourselves rather than through a booking agency. We could turn away people who sounded peculiar or difficult. This helped us avoid a further delicate problem: that of the tragic legion of elderly women who roam the holiday resorts of Britain in search of a permanent home. One evening I had just finished the skyscraper piles of washing up when the phone rang. A shrill woman's voice came over the wire after the pay phone pips had sounded.

"I want somewhere to stay tonight. There's just me and my well-trained King Charles spaniel. I've just sold my house and as I used to come to Hereford as a child I got on the train and came here. I want to stay with someone who isn't commercial, who doesn't do it for the money and where I could have a long stay."

Deerpark was clearly not the home port she was seeking. We definitely did not take dogs and we definitely were in it for the money. I said we were full up.

"Oh dear, I've nowhere to go. What shall I do?" The shrill voice sounded near despair.

I suggested Hereford county library with its accommodation list of hotels and guest houses. There was a pause and then a sharp intake of breath.

"I couldn't possibly do that." She replied in a shocked tone. "They won't let me take my little doggie in such places."

As I became more and more obviously pregnant, many of our guests even cleared the table after meals and brought the tray of dishes out to the kitchen. And I would not have survived without the help of a motherly visitor who almost took over the house when I was laid low for two agonising days after eating some suspect prawns, part of a Chinese takeaway meal which I had got Tom to collect from the nearby town to save me cooking our own meal. She elbowed me away from the sink after meals and gave me a welcome hand to clean up the house in the mornings.

Exhaustion, I realised, seemed to be the main hazard of running a guest house, even on a small scale as we were doing. Even worse was the need, indeed the extreme importance, of concealing that weariness from the guests. For nothing, I reckoned, is calculated to spoil people's enjoyment of a holiday more than the periodic appearance of a flushed, tired and overwrought landlady. However tired I felt, I knew I must not show it. The supreme test of my self-control arose over the activities of the more relentless of the visiting children. Clear leaders were the Parkinsons, who drove us to hitherto unrealised limits of self-restraint. They were on holiday with four of their six children, although most of the time it sounded as though there were at least a dozen of them. Feet pounded, voices shrieked as they leapt up and down stairs and raced along the passages. Figures tore in the front door, through the house and disappeared through the kitchen door, although the kitchen, the family's remaining living space, was officially out of bounds.

The youngest child, an eight-year-old called Jonathan, was another member of the hobgoblin species. He soon developed a hilarious game of approaching Tom's horse, Al, in the stable and clapping his hands suddenly. Being a high-spirited horse Al would rear up in alarm and bang his head on the beam above the stable door. Luckily we caught Jonathan at it before any harm was done and explained that he might think it was funny, but the horse did not. As we got to know Jonathan we realised that although he was cheeky, he was a likeable, cheerful child. The same could not be said of his fourteen-year-old sister, Joy. After the family's first night with us I was taken aback to find the skirting board in her room inscribed in indelible pencil with the word MICKLEMORE. It was a reminder that farm holidays seldom suit adolescents—and also a long way down to scrub when you are carrying an extra stone around the waist. Within a couple of days Joy made it glaringly obvious that she resented being forced to come on holiday with her younger brother and sisters. She would much rather have stayed at a seaside resort where there were cafés, discotheques and opportunities to meet boys. When her parents and younger siblings piled into the car and disappeared down the track with shrieks of enthusiasm, Joy was left with us. ("You don't mind if Joy stays on the farm, do you? It's so boring for her with the younger children.") We tried gently to organise things for her to do, but she still spent most of the holiday draped over the stable doors or leaning against the barn walls hoping to catch the eye of the one boy on the premises, a fifteen-year-old who sometimes helped out during weekends and school holidays. At mealtimes she refused much of the food with bad grace and afterwards listlessly searched the columns of the local paper for the times of the cinema performances in Hereford. I could understand how she felt, and indeed, disconsolate teenage girls were to be one of our main bugbears in the months to come. But she was hard going all the same.

Mr. and Mrs. Marshall, our next guests, had no children with them. Indeed, they were taking their first holiday away from their four children, the youngest of which, aged eight, had gone to stay with cousins. Mr. Marshall was a hospital administrator with, I suspect, a background in one of the armed services. He had a manner that was both commanding and persuasive. His wife had a very similar manner, and enough experience to make her an expert on life in its initial stages. Surprisingly she did not look like a mother of four children. There was no hint of the spreading girth and harassed manner you might expect. With her trim figure and calm features Mrs. Marshall was one of those enviable women who seem unmarked by a succession of pregnancies. At the time I certainly felt very marked by mine and Mrs. Marshall was not short of advice. This was not imparted in the manner of two women exchanging confidences; she dispensed advice to me as she would have done to the wives of 'other ranks', with friendliness and unchallengeable authority. To increase her position of command she usually delivered this advice when she was in a position of physical superiority, for instance, standing upright on the other side of the room while I grovelled on the floor sweeping the awkward bit of carpet under the sideboard.

She delivered her first pronouncement as I was laboriously brushing the stair carpet and she was leaning thoughtfully over the banisters along the upstairs passage.

"Are you sure the baby's not due until December? You haven't made a mistake with the dates? You're awfully big for five months. I never remember being your sort of size until I was at least seven months." She added with finality tinged with triumph at her own perceptiveness: "You must be carrying twins."

Her judgment sent a chill of fear through me. I am a

twin myself and my family is full of twins. There had been bad moments when I wondered despairingly how I would cope with one new baby as well as with Anthony. Twins would be a full-time job on their own. During that week I felt the baby's kicking anxiously. Could I feel two sets of football boots hammering away inside me? Or was it just one pair of fists and one pair of heels? Sometimes I feared it must be two babies, sometimes I convinced myself there was just one.

Mrs. Marshall had not finished frightening the life out of me. Two days later I was dusting the skirting board in the lounge when she delivered a really fast one.

"You're some way from the nearest hospital aren't you?"

"Oh no," I replied. "It's only fifteen miles to the County Hospital in Hereford."

Mrs. Marshall looked concerned. "Well, I do admire you. I'd have been scared to death if I'd lived in the middle of nowhere when I was pregnant. Of course they couldn't hope to get an ambulance up here. Aren't you worried that things might start happening when your husband is away at market or somewhere?"

Up till then I had never given the problem a thought. Our financial predicament had blotted out all such difficulties. Now I remembered how the child of a mother in the village possessed a birth certificate where the place of birth was recorded as: 'level crossing on the A.49 at Marlbrook'. That was the spot the ambulance had reached when the baby made its appearance. At least that mother had had an ambulance. All I had in case of an emergency was the phone number of a neighbour. It was a plan we had used when Anthony was due. Tom's absences then were always covered by one of our neighbours who agreed to be on standby for a few hours.

I worried and fretted until the Marshalls' last morning. A simple query cleared my mind. Mr. Marshall had just finished signing his cheque when he waved his arm expansively and asked: "Is all this your choice or what?" I looked round at the sitting room trying to understand what he was on about. It was not decorated and furnished in contemporary *Homes and Gardens* style. Tom and I had chosen curtains and lampshades with a hunting design to co-ordinate with Tom's plaques, with the three most cherished rosettes from his show-jumping days, and with two old hunting prints we owned. My leather Chesterfield fitted in naturally. The result was exactly what we wanted.

Mr. Marshall clarified his statement: "I mean, is all this 'décor' just for the benefit of the paying guests?"

I kept up the mien of the cheerful landlady until their car was out of sight. Then I turned to Tom:

"The Marshalls," I told him, "would benefit from some of John Hopkins' therapy for over-zealous insurance salesmen. Both of them."

After four months in the farm holiday trade we were beginning to realise that to most of our guests the farm played merely a secondary role. It was no more than a scenic background to a modest guest house. I was surprised at the number of people who never wanted to wander through the avenues of oaks on the front pasture, or to walk the few yards to our western boundary to gaze over the long sweep of the fertile fields of the Marches to the distant, watchful Welsh hills. A few people even tried to shut out the agricultural scene completely, drawing the living-room curtains tightly. The evening sunlight slanting through imposing oak trees, chickens pecking and scratching in the yard, kittens tumbling in play, all ceased to exist for them as they settled around the television. Sometimes a transistor radio was produced and Radio 1 blared out the latest pop tunes, jamming any of the farmyard noises that might penetrate the closed curtains.

But as the season reached its peak in August, our visitors tended to be younger and they often had children of school age. To our delight, some of these guests were eager to lend a hand on the farm in the long, light summer evenings. Our problem was to find any way in which they could help. On most farms nowadays there is little call for unskilled muscle-power. Mechanisation means that the days when visitors to the countryside could join in the life and work of the farms are almost over. Haymaking, for instance, used to be an occasion when everyone, young and old, turned out in the fields to turn the sweet-smelling grasses with forks and rakes, to pitch it into the great hay wains, and fork it off again on to the stacks. Today it is mostly a one-man job performed by a single tractor pulling a lethal, whirring tedder. Even the warm fragrance of the crop is little more than a memory. The sweet vernal, meadow fescues have been overwhelmed by the more vigorous but less fragrant species encouraged by artificial fertilisers. At harvest time there is no reaper and binder for children to follow in the hope of clobbering luckless rabbits with sticks and stones—and there are far fewer rabbits anyway. Now monster combine harvesters with their satellite grain trailers tackle the job and there is hardly a person on foot to be seen in the vast, lonely fields.

Only in late summer and autumn can visitors embark on their own hedgerow harvest and take their farm holiday to its logical conclusion by collecting their own food, scouring the fields in the early mornings for mushrooms and struggling through thick curtains of thorns for blackberries, crab apples and wild cherries.

Where manpower is used on the modern farm what is wanted is skilled manpower. It is easy to think that all that is needed to tackle most jobs on the land is sheer brute force combined with enthusiasm. Yet there is real skill in almost every job on a farm from handling bales, or loading a trailer, or shifting heavy bags of fertiliser to cornering a calf and giving it an injection.

We found however that on a small farm like Deerpark, where machines have not yet triumphed over muscle-power, we could still find some work for the willing and eager. A family of four helped Tom get in our entire winter supply of logs, loading on to the trailer the wood which Tom had sawn from one of the ash trees killed by the drought. They then turned willingly to collecting the brushwood into heaps to be burnt. Another family gamely tackled the deep litter in the calf boxes, forking the heavy, matted straw into barrows for wheeling to the muck heap. When the weather brightened and the grain harvest got under way at last, a young couple helped us cart the straw from the fields of a neighbouring farm. We had bought the right to bale the straw there after the combine harvester had finished reaping. The husband, Jack, had worked on a farm several years before and he volunteered to drive one of the tractors. They left the house in high spirits and returned in high dudgeon.

Jack looked both cross and sheepish. His wife Jane just glowered.

"What on earth is up with them?" I asked Tom when he appeared. "You didn't push them too hard, did you?" I had vivid memories of the builder Tom had employed the previous year at the rate of £1.50 an hour. Tom had 'organised' him and for ten days a resentful Rumplestiltskin figure had doubled round the yard with a wheelbarrow full of cement, a bucket of plaster or an armful of timber.

Tom shook his head and laughed. "Didn't you hear the row? You missed a rare old ding-dong. He *said* he could drive a tractor, but when he came through the top gate by the house with the loaded trailer he turned too sharply under the oak and the low branch swept off the top layer of bales and swept off his missus who was sitting on top of the lot. She was not pleased."

That had been Jack and Jane's last day. We still had the bulk of the 1600 bales of straw to bring in. It was the most exhausting of the summer jobs at Deerpark. We tried to hire some help, but everyone else in the area was at full stretch harvesting their own crops after the long delay which the bad weather had caused. Finally Tom managed to enlist one helper, our neighbour Joan, a slip of a girl who worked in the Gritty Grains health food shop when the field work was slow. We were lucky, because she was a real worker, even though she looked as if she could barely lift a sheaf of corn, let alone a forty-pound bale of straw.

Then fate intervened and our farming and holiday activities came together in a way marvellously beneficial to both. The form fate took was of a family from the north of England, the Martins, in search not only of a holiday in the south, but of an energetic holiday. From the moment I spotted their blue Saab racing up the track—the Martins did everything with verve—I had a feeling we were in for a good week. George Martin was six feet six inches of muscle and jokes, with a prodigious appetite for work and an instinctive skill at getting other people not only to take on gruelling tasks, but to enjoy them. His wife Joyce was a small woman who said very little, but who could shift almost as much work as her powerful husband. With their two lithe teenage daughters, they made a formidable team—and they were dying to help on the farm.

They made that plain on the first morning of their holiday. Instead of asking me which were the best places to visit nearby, they wanted to know what was happening on the farm. When I told them we were baling and carting in the straw, they asked their way to the field and turned up there soon after breakfast. Tom was towing the baler behind the tractor and Joan was walking behind stacking the bales into compact groups of six from which they could be loaded on to the trailer for hauling to the big barn behind the house.

George Martin wasted no time. "You need a bit of northern muscle here," he said. "You southerners"—this with a broad grin—"have got a lot to learn about real work." With that he hung his jacket on one pile of bales and started to sling the next pile on to the waiting trailer. Without delay his wife and daughters followed his lead.

Joan counselled caution. She had had years of experience of straw harvesting, and had seen many an enthusiastic novice run out of energy after the first hour. "Take it easy," she warned, "we're going to be doing this all day. Each one of these bales weighs at least forty pounds. The temperature out here will be in the eighties by mid-day. When we start stacking them under the corrugated-iron roof of the barn it will be over a hundred. You've got to conserve your energy at this job."

George was not daunted. "That may be so for you southerners. Where we come from work really means something."

He was as good as his word. Right through that long hot day he kept at this self-appointed task. When his children faltered and took occasional breaks on the nearest bale of straw, he cursed them cheerfully and loudly. No southern woman was going to show up his family. When by mid-afternoon they began to complain at the pace, he would hear none of it. "*She's* still at it," he said, pointing to Joan. His tone was no doubt much the same as that of the officer in the Peninsula War against Napoleon's Spanish allies, who urged on his troops to the attack with the words: "Are you fellows who eat beef going to be beaten by this lot who live on oranges?"

By the tea break George's appearance worried Joan. He looked grey with weariness. He was used to hard work, but not to the glare of the sun coming off a field of stubble. He had a blinding headache. He spurned the offer of an aspirin, but accepted the loan of Tom's Mexican straw hat, and returned to the trailer 'to work it off'.

I got them back into the house for supper and managed to disengage the girls. But George and Joyce were off after the meal to collect one more load. They then rounded off the day recharging their batteries at the Fox and Pheasant, so conveniently situated at the end of our farm lane. By the time they made their way up our bumpy road, to collapse in sleep regardless of a harvest moon that shone directly on to their bedroom window, they had become part of Micklebury. The next day they were down in the field again after breakfast, sharing a laugh with Joan and keeping up the pace right through to the evening. When finally all 1600 bales were stacked in the barn, they surveyed the result with satisfaction and were prepared to agree that Joan might well have been a northerner, the way she worked. Joan confided to me, "I've never come across a family like them. Nothing stops them. I thought at one point that George was going to collapse under the heat, but he just went on chucking up bales on to the trailer."

The Martins' help was for us a double bonus. Not only had the terrible slog of the harvest been lightened, but we had a family of guests who were delighted to have really tasted farming life. The comradeship and cheerfulness which comes from successfully carrying out a job together spread through the house. For a few days we had experienced the harvest as our forebears must have experienced it. The Martins took this for granted, as a normal part of country life. This is what they had read about, what they had come to the country to find. I was deeply thankful that they had come at one of the few times in the farming year when such an experience could be shared by all.

On the final evening of their holiday, Tom took George and Joyce down to the Fox and Pheasant for a thank-you drink. It was four in the morning before they returned. The next morning George was dull-eyed and grey-faced. He came to the breakfast table shaking his head as if trying to clear a buzzing from his ears.

"Oof. I can keep up with Tom working. But I can't keep up with his playing."

# A bad sale

I had my niggling doubts about our last guests of the season when they booked. They sounded perhaps a little too frail for the robust life at Deerpark. But they wanted the last week of our season so I decided to take the chance. Even if the week was a disaster I would have the whole winter to recover.

The Egans, as they were called, arrived on a sunny September Saturday, a day when the farm appeared both bright and beautiful. Warm strong sunlight flooded through the full foliage of the oak trees and glowed on grass which was still emerald, with no hint of the rank yellow that would creep into it with the progress of autumn. The farm was at its best; a summer of warmth and peace had healed the raw wounds of winter. The muddy quagmires by the gates were green with soft turf; gaping holes in the hedges had been filled with fresh new growth; even the potholes in the road had disappeared. But the Egans were immune to Deerpark's glories. From the moment their car pulled up on the yard, my welcoming words were met with a tirade of complaints about the bumps in the road. I knew we were in for a long and difficult week.

As I had guessed the Egans were a frail couple and the first problem was to convey their suitcases from the foot of the stairs to the top of the stairs. Tom was over a mile away carting straw for neighbours, I was too pregnant, Mrs. Egan refused in principle and Mr. Egan was obviously in very poor health. I suggested they wait for Tom but Mr. Egan, at his wife's insistence, toiled up and down the stairs with the cases, panting like a man about to breathe his last. Between puffs he explained that he only had one lung, because the other had been removed three years before when he was suffering from cancer. I did my best to fuss around them, showing them where the extra blankets were kept, asking them if they wanted a cup of tea or coffee or if they would like the heating turned up.

They ate the evening meal in silence and went to bed early. The next morning I asked them if they slept well, if everything was all right.

"We were so cold," complained Mrs. Egan. "We had to go to bed."

"I'm so sorry," I apologised. "Why didn't you turn on the electric fire?" I motioned to the electric fire sitting prominently in the fireplace.

Mrs. Egan shook her head doubtfully. "We didn't like to, dear."

I was further convinced that they were people who were impossible to please when they returned to the farm at three o'clock in the afternoon the following day, Sunday.

"Hello. Did you have a nice day?" I tried to force some cheerfulness into my voice, although I was depressed by the prospect of having such a manifestly unhappy couple around the house for the rest of the afternoon.

Mr. Egan looked gloomy. "Not really. We had a look round Leominster, but all the shops were closed."

As the week progressed they grew no happier. At mealtimes if I popped my head round the door to see if they were ready for the next course, and they had not yet finished, Mrs. Egan would remonstrate with her husband in a shrill voice:

"I told you so. I *told* you. I said if you didn't hurry up and eat your cornflakes she'd bring in the next course before you had finished."

It began to get very unnerving. Try as I could, I never seemed to judge the right moment. Either they were still eating, or were sitting resentfully in front of emptied plates. On Wednesday I was cleaning the bath when I heard a scream. There was a pause and then Mr. Egan spoke:

"We'll have to tell her. He shouldn't do that." I rushed, or rather because of my bulk, lumbered outside. My son, who has a poor sense of timing, had added a further complication by throwing a piece of brick at Mrs. Egan. It had fallen well short, but it was hardly a welcoming gesture.

Daily I became more tense and nervous. But the Egans, for their part, seemed to be beginning to relax a little. Mr. Egan, as he unwound, explained the trouble bit by bit. His wife, devastated by his illness, had had an attack of severe depression and had been in a mental hospital until the month before.

"Our neighbour—he's dead now: we went to his funeral the day before we came away—showed us your advertisement. It looked just the thing. Mrs. Egan is too nervous to go to a hotel but she really needed a holiday." He sighed and shook his head sadly.

"It's been so difficult. All the way here she thought the car was going to break down. She worries all the time that things will go wrong."

I began to be more and more influenced by Mrs. Egan's state of mind. Every time their car trundled down the road the exhaust emitted a series of loud snorts. All we needed was for their exhaust to fall off. One evening I glanced out of the window to see Anthony sitting astride the exhaust pipe bouncing up and down on it. I chased him off, and crossed my finger that the exhaust would remain attached, however tenuously, to their car, until they left. If it dropped off Mrs. Egan's nerves would have a field day.

To my great relief the exhaust stayed put. Indeed by the end of the week Mrs. Egan was beginning to look distinctly perky. But it was not my efforts that affected the real transformation of Mrs. Egan's outlook on life. The turning point was on Friday evening when she returned to the farm in triumph bearing a loaf of bread. There was a bread strike on at the time. The television news had shown pictures of people in towns queueing for bread from five in the morning. The Egans had met a baker's van on their travels and had stopped it and bought a loaf. That simple purchase changed Mrs. Egan's demeanour completely. I had the feeling that she believed she had at last thwarted the hostile fates determined to do her down. She radiated a sudden, and very attractive, cheerfulness. Indeed she announced that they had enjoyed their holiday so much they would like to stay an extra day. When they confined their complaints that evening to a protest that the steaks I served them were far too big for their modest appetites, I took this as a sign of appreciation, not rebuke.

Nevertheless, I heaved a sigh of relief when the Egans' car, its exhaust still blurting and shaking, made its way for the last time cautiously down the farm track. That was that. Our first season as a guest house was over—and just in time. The baby was due in just over two months. I could not face even one further day of cooking and cleaning for paying guests. Now our home was our own again, at least for the winter months. It had been harder work than I had ever anticipated but our bank balance had received a live-saving blood transfusion. We had indeed had an experience very rare for farmers. We had been gathering for six months a steady cash crop, with money moving each week into our bank account. We had got through to the autumn without having to sell cattle prematurely. We had survived. Whether we had done more than just survive depended now upon the most important event of our farming year—the sale of the cattle.

If we got a good price, then we would need to borrow less for next year, and would be the richer by the amount of the lower interest we would pay to the bank. If we got a bad price, then we must work through yet another year carrying a full burden of debts.

Early in September we had already sold one bunch of ten of the largest heifers. Although the price per hundredweight had been lower than we had hoped—below the level of the previous year—the cattle had gained far more weight than we had expected and we had been happy with the price we had received for them. It was now the beginning of October and we had to sell most of the rest of our beef cattle by the beginning of November. The reason for our haste was that Hereford Market would not accept 'unaccredited' cattle after that. The county was in the middle of clearing brucellosis—an unpleasant and highly infectious disease—from its herds. Not only does the disease cause abortion in cows, but humans can also catch it from them and suffer symptoms that resemble a combination of arthritis and malaria. One vet in six in the area had had brucellosis. Our own farm seemed unaffected and was in the middle of a programme of being tested by Ministry experts for a certificate of clearance. We would, however, not be completely cleared for several more months. We had the choice of selling our cattle in October whilst unaccredited cattle were still acceptable, or waiting until after Christmas when our accreditation would—with luck—come through.

Selling day is always a nerve-wracking time. The result

of a whole year's work—all the feeding, mucking out, dosing for worms, washing for lice, all the work on the pastures—is crammed into a minute or two when the cattle appear in the sale ring. With our hearts in our mouths we listen to the bids: not only profit or loss for the whole year, but our prospects for the following year all hinge on those precious seconds. Prices can vary from week to week. They can even alter drastically overnight. The market for meat is one of the few that is still determined by supply and demand, and prices depend on a whole host of factors—bank interest rates, feed prices, the stability of the government, the policies of other members of the Common Market. Hot weather and school holidays cut the demand for beef and reduce the price of animals of all ages except calves. During haymaking and harvest times farmers may not have time to attend the weekly market and prices may ease. On a wet day, in contrast, farmers may decide to have a day out and the bidding will be keen. If prices rise the effect can be infectious. Buyers are often caught up in the general enthusiasm for buying cattle, on the basis:

"Trade's good, better buy now before prices rise even more."

The actions of foreign governments also affect us quickly and sharply. Decisions taken in Brussels about the Irish green pound or the Italian green lira will have an immediate effect on the personal finances of farmers like us standing around the sale ring of Hereford Market.

If the trade is diabolical it is, of course, possible to withdraw the cattle from the sale and take them home. But they will have lost condition in the process. The trip to market, the stress of standing around tightly packed in pens all day takes its toll. Cattle can lose up to half a hundredweight each in the course of such a day. This fact must be balanced against the lower prices.

So we face market days with considerable apprehension. And on that selling day in October our normal fears were intensified by an early morning radio report that cattle markets throughout the country were showing weakness. As the cattle scrambled up the ramp of the lorry Tom and I marvelled at how well they looked. The scraggy pot-bellied animals that had waited so patiently at the farmyard gate in May had metamorphosised into big, sturdy, glossy heifers. We hoisted up the ramp and screwed up the bolts. By the time we climbed into the cab a thin drizzle began to seep from the miserable grey sky. Lurching down the drive we could feel that winter was on the way. Gradually the surface of the track was opening up again—it was the start of the pothole season.

When we reached the market all signs of the summer had disappeared. The drizzle had thickened into a thin penetrating rain and the town was blanketed in an uncomfortable dampness; that cold autumn rain that seems to soak your very soul. It made our noses drip, it crept down our coat collars and rose up from the slushing concrete ground through the leather soles of our boots. More water worked its way insidiously through the creases in our coats at the elbows and our trousers at the knees.

If the weather was unpleasant the state of the market was even worse. Prices had crashed. Bullocks were making barely £30 a hundredweight, heifers £27, which was about ten per cent less than the previous year. Archie Daws, a contractor whose business was carrying stock to and from market, had one explanation; Irish cattle, attracted by a Common Market subsidy which they got, but our cattle did not, were pouring into Britain and depressing the market price. Archie himself had contracts to transport hundreds of Irish beasts every week from Holyhead to a slaughterhouse in Devon.

It seemed the supreme irony of the Common

Market—or rather of the terms which the British government was imposing on our own farmers as part of the price of our entry. Irish agriculture, once regarded as a joke, was crushing British livestock farming, and crushing it with the help of subsidies of which the British taxpayer met a major share. In the years that followed the Republic of Eire's entry into the Common Market, the incomes of their farmers had trebled. They had done so because prices for the produce of Irish farms averaged twenty percent more than those which the British farmer received. To cap it all, the Irish were moving into British farms. Land in Ireland could fetch up to £3,000 an acre, as against a price of £1,500—£2,000 an acre for comparable land here. It was no wonder that the grass seemed greener this side of the Irish Channel.

All we could do was to try and ensure that we secured the best price of the day for our cattle. For there are some steps which a farmer can take to help his cattle to sell well. If he can offer them in bunches of ten or a dozen animals, the price can well be several pounds above that which they will fetch as single beasts. Appearance counts too. We knew that, since we used our own lorry to carry our stock, they would arrive at the market looking fresh. They would not have been squashed so tightly together that they would reach market having covered each other with manure—a thing cattle are particularly adept at doing. We also arranged the journey so that the cattle had to spend as little time as possible standing in the pens. This meant not only that they looked better when they trotted into the ring, they also weighed a bit more because the contents of their stomachs were still inside them, not distributed ankle deep on the floor of the pens.

Even so, our proud and beautiful heifers were soon a sorry sight. They had to be penned in the open, in the rain. Within fifteen minutes they looked wet and miserable, standing with their heads bowed as the rain slid off the dying leaves of the horse-chestnut trees that ringed the pens.

But the most important thing was to indicate to prospective buyers that ours were 'farmers' cattle'. Many of the animals which pass through a large market like Hereford are sold by dealers who attend the smaller markets along the Welsh border. They buy up small lots of cattle, match them into larger bunches and re-sell them at major markets. These 'dealer's cattle' may have spent the previous few days standing in draughty markets, or touring the countryside in livestock lorries, and therefore, tend to take some time to settle down. Many buyers prefer to buy cattle that have come straight off a farm that morning.

Up to about five years ago farmers would spend the time before the sale smartening up their cattle for the ring, washing them down and grooming their coats with an old scrubbing brush. Now, not many people bother to give their animals a wash and brush up. The sudden lurches of price resulting from political as well as remote economic forces, make such final touches seem irrelevant.

Tom and I were studying our heifers intently when two men approached us. They stood out from the farming folk in the market; bland faces, smooth and untanned from the sun and wind; baggy but expensive tweed slacks descending into shiny green army surplus Wellingtons that had never seen service in a muddy field in mid-winter. Butchers. Even today, when almost everything is not only mass-produced but also mass-marketed through chain stores, there are still many family butchers in country towns who buy and kill their own cattle. A few, like the two men interested in our heifers, were accustomed to finishing the fattening process on their own fields to exactly the size of beast their customers might want. They looked the cattle over, ummed and ahed and grunted. Finally they faced Tom.

"Nice bunch of cattle. Did you rear them yourselves?"
Tom nodded. Then the taller of the butchers asked:
"How much luck money will you give us?"
Luck money is a token, usually a pound or two, given by the seller to the buyer. It always struck me as a singularly inappropriate practice when the market was low. Not only did it have to come out of the auction price, but if your luck with the animals was clearly lousy, why transfer any takings to the buyer?

But the question indicated that the butchers would bid for the cattle, and that meant they should fetch a little more than the average for the day. Most of the lots were bought by dealers. Animals which attracted bids from farmers or butchers normally sold at a premium.

Our cattle were amongst the last lots in the catalogue and the wet weary day dragged on. At last our cattle clattered into the ring. Tom stood in the auctioneer's box giving instructions on the reserve. On the illuminated board on the sale ring the weight of the beasts flashed up. I did some quick calculations; the heifers averaged seven hundredweight. We had hoped they would fetch about £210 apiece. I knew that was ridiculously optimistic now. Some animals of that weight were only making £185. The bidding was slow: £150 . . . £155 . . . £160. It crept up to £180, with only an extra pound being added to each bid. At £187 it seemed to be 'all up' when the butcher at last spoke up. The price edged up to £194 each. I sighed with relief and nodded my support to Tom in the auctioneer's box. The hammer came down and the heifers belonged to the butchers. The next lot of eight made £175. Tom looked across for my view. I shook my head. The hammer came down. "All done!" shouted the auctioneer. That group were still ours. Finally our last animal came into the ring, a single red heifer we called Nellie, who was smaller than the others. The top bid was £130 —only £5 more than we had paid for her in February. We wearily withdrew her too from the auction.

I picked Anthony up and went to find Tom outside the auction ring. The rain-swept marketplace was empty. The day had not been a total disaster. At least the butchers' intervention had saved us taking all the cattle home. But it was bad enough. Tom and I looked at each other near to despair. Our hopes that we would have cleared enough to ensure a better year the following season were dashed. Not much mental arithmetic was needed to see we would be severely short of money again, that once again we would get by only on a costly overdraft. With a sinking heart I knew there was now no question of taking visitors only in the peak school holiday period in the coming year. Handicapped by a tiny baby, we would have to do the full season. More than that we would have to double our takings from tourism if we were to see any long term future at Deerpark. Suddenly I felt very tired, very wet and very pregnant. Tom took my free hand.

"There's no point in thinking about it. That's just the way things go."

# Closed season

Winter closed in on us quickly. The evenings grew darker and the trees shed their leaves so suddenly that within a few days the flaming screen of orange and gold foliage that had protected the east and west flanks of the farm gave way to a black picket of bare trees. The old leaves gathered in heaps in corners by the farm buildings, the forlorn litter of the lavish summer. Sometimes a sharp flurry of autumn winds swept them together and threw them into our faces with handfuls of stinging dust as we drew our coats around us and hurried about the jobs outside. Out on the pastures the grass stopped pushing through the rich red earth and the ground was soon a carpet of matted bleached growth.

Yet autumn at Deerpark has a way of going out with a flourish. There was a magical, almost supernatural quality about those shortening days. Morning mists swirled low over the fields and hedgerows, enveloping them in a veil of dampness. As the sun gradually forced its way through the fog, the atmosphere cleared and first the tree tops, then the larger bushes and finally the fields emerged like Atlantis from the sea. The dawn mists condensed on the fine, intricate cobwebs that were strung across the grass, suspended from the hedges, even wound round the washing line and draped over the iron frame of the windmill above the well. Indeed everything seemed to be covered with these gossamer filaments as though nature itself was weaving a spell over our surroundings to keep them cocooned until the warm spring winds breathed life into the countryside the following April.

The days when the house was full of noisy holiday-makers, and when we had flung open the doors and windows to let in the sunshine, seemed ages ago, as we stuffed draught-excluder foam in the gaps round the window-frames, and stacked logs for the fires. Our two spare rooms now housed the quite considerable array of clothes and equipment that is needed by a new baby. How we were going to organise for the holiday season the following summer a household containing this new-comer, was a matter Tom and I had not considered yet. But clearly he or she would not have the luxury of a room to itself—the spare rooms would all be needed for the paying guests.

Even in the depths of winter we could not forget completely our role as proprietors of Deerpark Guest House. One mucky November night when the back kitchen was swamped with slushy mud from our Wellingtons and an icy wind was whistling under the doors, we heard a sudden outburst of furious barking from our Alsation, Zara, as we were having tea. Zara is a faithful and devoted dog, but one who is not blessed with great intelligence. Her job is to be a watchdog, to sound the alarm and if necessary to attack suspicious strangers. She sounded the alarm with great efficiency if any of the stock escaped, barking in an unmistakable frenzy. But strangers presented more of a problem because she was unable to distinguish between friend and foe, and tended to give few people the benefit of the doubt. In her zealousness to defend us she was apt to believe that attack was the best form of defence.

So when guests were around, we had no choice but to

lock our over-enthusiastic security guard in a stable, letting her out during the night. Now the guests were gone Zara was making up for lost time. As we heard the deep-throated barks we wondered idly which of the tabby cats was running for its life. Then we heard a more identifiable sound.

"Arrang, arrah, arrah."

I put my mug of tea down and for a split second my eyes met Tom's. He had the same thought. We both leapt up. I dived for the back door and shoved my feet into my waiting Wellingtons. Tom grabbed his shotgun. Strangers did not call unannounced at remote farms like Deerpark at five o'clock on a November evening unless they had some sinister motive. That is why we needed a guard dog. Hearts pounding, we flung open the back door.

Through the rain and blackness I could discern the figure of a man, the corner of his jacket firmly trapped between Zara's teeth. Behind him I could make out an unassuming black Morris 1100. The man waved a card at me.

"I'm the registrations officer from the Heart of England Tourist Board.

"Ask him for his identification," hissed Tom behind me.

That, I thought, would indeed add insult to the injury he had already sustained from Zara's teeth.

"We thought you were the Black Panther," I explained lamely.

The officer was shaken but not angry. Perhaps it was one of the accepted hazards of the job. "That's all right. No harm done. I called because we just like to see where people are, you know."

I led the way into the house, through the muddy kitchen and up the stairs littered with the wisps of straw that always find their way into farmhouses during the winter. I showed off my letting bedrooms, both icy-cold, dusty and full of baby things.

"They are not normally like this," I tried to explain, feeling extremely flustered. "I'm having a baby next month."

I went on. "And the guests come in through the front door not through the kitchen as you did, but we cover the door with a sheet of polythene during the winter to stop the draughts."

I must stop apologising, I thought. I must act confidently. I took a deep breath and opened the living-room door. That too had its full share of winter clutter. "This is the lounge—I serve meals in here too. Oh, the table isn't usually covered in papers; I was just doing our VAT returns."

The man from the tourist board showed no surprise. It was clear that his job had given him a realistic view of farming behind the scenes.

"Oh, that's fine. This isn't an inspection. We just like to see who's doing what, where they are and so on. But now I must dash. I've got to be in Ross at five thirty." He turned down our offer of a drink and, a minute later, the Morris 1100 roared to life and wooshed down the lane through the puddles in the potholes, accompanied by the cacophony of frustrated barking from Zara, backed by Lyn, the border collie and by Risky, the Jack Russell terrier.

I looked ruefully at Zara, wondering whether she had earned for us an indelible black mark. But we heard no more from the tourist board about the incident. Three months later we received a handsome card inscribed REGISTERED WITH THE ENGLISH TOURIST BOARD. I covered it carefully with plastic, ready to give it pride of place on our front door.

The baby was not the only newcomer expected on the farm. Our heifer, Bambi, was at last in calf. But now it was the turn of her mother, Angel, our much-loved house cow, to have difficulty in conceiving. The assistance of modern science was enlisted again, but to no avail. The monthly vet's bill spelt out the battery of treatment she was receiving; hormone injections to bring her into season, more injections to make her hold. And still she was barren.

"If she won't conceive we will have to get rid of her. She's to have no more injections or anything." Tom pronounced the conditions of Angel's reprieve from the death sentence. "If she comes into season she will be inseminated. We'll keep her until this lactation is over, but if she's not in calf when her milk dries up, she'll have to go into the market."

He did not like the idea any more than I did. I had become used to the harsher aspects of keeping animals for profit. There is no room on a small farm to allow barren cows an idle and early retirement. As long as cows are productive they live in comfort. But once they stop producing an annual calf and milk which accompanies it, they have to go. There is a strong market for barren cows, which are in demand for meat for frozen food products, pies and puddings. The demand is such that big Friesian cows make only 10p a pound less than prime beef cattle.

Angel was already living on borrowed time. She was a delicate cow. From the day she had arrived at the farm three years before at the age of two and a half she had been a regular patient of our local vet. On a dairy farm an animal like her would have been weeded out years ago. But she was a gentle, affectionate cow; in good health she produced six gallons a day of thick, creamy milk and was a good foster mother to the calves we put on her.

After Tom's pronouncement I went out to the cowshed and rubbed the top of her head where the hay seeds collected. She regarded me with her deep brown eyes and responded by rubbing her head on my sleeve. I was not milking her at that period because I was so pregnant. Angel seemed to know when I was in that state, and it seemed to worry her. Normally when she was milked she stood stock still as I drew the creamy milk from her small neat teats. But as soon as I grew large and awkward and had difficulty getting up and down from the low three-legged milking stool Angel became restless, moving a few steps one way and then the other. This gave me the choice of milking her at arms length or of going through the laborious operation of moving the stool. Angel would turn her head from the manger and watch my manoeuvres with a glint in her eyes which you could interpret as murderous laughter or as a warning that truly pregnant women ought not to be milking.

On misty nights Angel had another ploy. Instead of waiting at the gate as she usually did when we called her in after dark, there would be no sign of her. Tom and I would call and shout and then, fearing she had found a hole in a hedge and wandered off to other pastures, we would tramp off round the perimeter of the field. Still there would be no sign of Angel. Only when we had completed the twenty-minute walk and arrived back, would we find her standing at the farmyard gate. As we strode towards her, our panting breaths creating small clouds of fog in the misty night air, the beams of our torches would spotlight that teasing, mischievous glint.

I shuddered at the prospect of selling our lovely cow in the market. Often I had seen the old cows standing forlornly in the iron pens under the chestnut trees in Hereford and had wondered how anyone could be so heartless as to allow animals they had cared for over the years, with names and individual habits and quirks to end their days so ignominiously. But we certainly could not afford a pensioner in our fields, and so now we were thinking of doing the same thing. Angel, however, had other ideas. Just as we were getting up our resolution to take her to market, she started to come into season naturally, and eventually conceived.

Shortly afterwards I had my own obstetric event. In keeping with rural tradition, Tom and I found ourselves hurtling along the empty country roads on a dark, still night, in an eighty-mile-an-hour dash to the hospital many miles away. The baby, a boy weighing over nine pounds, was born several hours later without any fuss. We gave him the straightforward country name of William, and life lost no time in resuming its usual eventful course. Two days after my return from hospital, the gusting winds that pounded us regularly now that the wood to the west had been thinned, swept a block of slates off the timbered roof.

We fetched ladders and ropes. The new baby's rattle proved to be just the thing to attach to a string, which in turn was tied to a rope and then thrown over the house to pull the ladder on to the roof.

"Never mind," remarked Tom cheerfully, "If the baby cries at least we can hear him through the hole in the roof."

No sooner was the roof repaired than winter hit us full force. Though it was to be outdone by the bitter winter of 1978–1979, this was the severest winter for many years. In Herefordshire we missed the worst of it. We watched on television on New Year's Eve the film of blizzards which blotted out Scotland where several people died, trapped in deep drifts. Other films showed hundreds of cattle and thousands of sheep which perished on upland farms. Only when the arctic weather returned at the end of February were we more directly affected; snow-blocked roads cut Deerpark off from the world for several days. Tom and I were thankful we had sold our flock of sheep and that all our animals were housed in warm barns and loose boxes. We were well stocked with food, so we rushed through the jobs outside, stuffed more draught excluder round the window-frames and watched the dramas of life in snowbound Britain on the television.

We watched with interest Denis Howell, the genial, avuncular Minister of Sport who had become a very familiar figure to farmers when he was appointed Minister of Drought and then Minister of Floods in 1976, come to prominence again as Minister of Snow to co-ordinate rescue services. A commercial salesman of women's underwear survived for 72 hours in a snowdrift by poking a pipe up through the snow and donning his stock of ladies' tights. A retired doctor in the West Country skied six miles to deliver a baby when the mother was unable to get to hospital for a Caesarian operation. I was doubly thankful my own son had been punctual enough to forestall this weather.

Night after night the temperature dropped off the bottom of the thermometer. Our new deep-frozen world had a strange, icy fascination. At night, and indeed sometimes during the day, it was so cold that our windows double-glazed themselves with a layer of ice on the inside of the panes. These ice panels were etched with weird figures and forms. As I washed up, the steam from the water froze on to the scullery windows to form an arctic still-life of trees and flowers. In other lights the ice was a mass of glittering stars and flashing diamonds. Sometimes the figures seemed almost animate; men kneeling, women washing, horses' heads, prehistoric animals—dinocerases and dinosaurs lumbering across our kitchen window-panes.

During the shuddering cold days and nights of late February the farm became a magnet for the wild animals in the countryside around us. All life drew closer together for protection. The perky robin that supervised the work on the farmyard, spent even more time perched on the handle of a fork or spade. Bluetits tut-tutted as they swung on the handle of the dog's food bucket that hung on the wall outside the kitchen. Hungry hordes of sparrows swooped on corn spilt on the yard, and blackbirds, thrushes and coaltits homed in on wheelbarrows of manure to sort through the muck for undigested corn. For a change, the birds were safe from their traditional foe, the farmyard cats. Our feline labour force had taken up residence on the kitchen doorstep like bargain hunters waiting for the first day of the sales. They lined up hoping to nip into the house for an illegal snack whenever the door opened.

Out in the pastures we could see the foraging, feeding, leaping and running figures of rabbits, squirrels and hares. Against the snow their brown coats were no longer an effective camouflage. Their activities were recorded in the criss-cross of hundreds of footprints in the snow. The sheer number of animal tracks surprised me. The fields seemed to have been as busy as Victoria Station in the rush hour. Perhaps the wild animals were the true tenants of the farm and we the intruders. Our occasional ventures across their territory were probably as much a surprise to them as the occasional glimpse of squirrels and rabbits on the pastures were to us.

Tom and I set out to see what the foxes were up to and to look for signs of the badgers that normally resided in the bank in the wood. To our surprise we could find no trace of these larger animals. Was it, we wondered sadly, the first real indication that the practice of snaring foxes, which had become common over the previous two winters, was affecting their numbers? We knew the local hunt had already drawn the wood twice that season and each time drawn a blank. Fox hunting is so often spoken of only as a sport—and as an anathema—that town dwellers overlook the fact that it is the normal method of controlling foxes in the countryside. There are other methods. In some areas like Wales, where the terrain is too rough for hounds, or in woodlands leased by shooting syndicates, the foxes are shot or snared. Many shooting syndicates indeed ban the hunts from their woods altogether. The sudden arrival of forty large hounds sniffing and crashing about in the undergrowth frightens off the game birds and ruins the sport for the shooters the following weekend. Gamekeepers too, who may rear hundreds of game chicks each spring, also guard their tiny charges assiduously, usually using snares to get rid of the foxes.

These long-established methods had over the years struck a rough balance and had maintained the fox population at a level which kept the hunts busy and the foxes reasonably in check. But now the balance was endangered, not by the agitation against fox hunting, but by the fact that everything in the countryside has its price, and the price of fox skins was no exception. For years there had been a steady, specialised market for fox pelts, chiefly as a source of materials for the manufacture of flies for fishing. The fur and feather dealers buy many types of game. They pay 2p for a pair of starling wings, 15p for jay wings, 5p for a squirrel tail, 12p for a mole skin. At the time we moved to Deerpark such dealers were the chief buyers of fox skins, for which they paid about £2 apiece. Four years later the situation had completely changed. Those with fox skins for sale found themselves in a different league altogether. The spread of rabies on the Continent meant that curers and furriers were extremely reluctant to handle European skins for fear of contracting the dreadful disease. As a result a huge demand had developed for British fox skins. The price leapt tenfold and dealers were paying upwards of £20 apiece for them. The British fur trade refused to use home grown fox pelts, declaring the pelts to be of inferior quality, but abroad they were in demand at the international fur auctions in Copenhagen. They went to make coats, scarves, collars and muffs, particularly in Germany and Italy. Frequently now the Sunday colour supplements show photographs of gorgeous girls in fur coats with the unmistakable lanky red fur of the British fox.

Not surprisingly the high prices led to a huge increase in the amount of fox snaring. Around Micklebury everyone seemed to be at it—not only gamekeepers but hard-pressed farmers making a bit of extra money for Christmas, and children earning extra pocket money for the school holidays. Poachers laid snares on seldom-visited waste land and old quarries. Although shooting tends to damage and mar the furs with blood, members of shooting syndicates are not above joining in, and organise fox-shooting Saturdays at the beginning and end of the season. It provides a bit of extra sport and a bit of extra cash.

Out of interest I wrote off to some of the larger dealers asking for their brochures. These were full of clear instructions. There was no great art to drying the skins. All you had to do was stretch them on a board, using ordinary pins. The skins could even be sent off while still wet. The dealers provided pre-addressed labels, details of Post Office parcels rates and British Rail rates for larger consignments. (How large I wondered?) They would even collect skins in their own vans. One dealer boasted that the previous year he had added over a thousand new suppliers of fox and mink skins to his existing list of several thousand suppliers. The trade was clearly quite considerable. What is worrying about it is that when there is an economic reason for killing animals, they die out quickly: in the countryside commercialism kills.

Tom and I are not great fox lovers. The previous year when one marauding fox was dining daily on my chickens I would have killed it instantly if I could. But we try to live at peace with the animals around us. We know that if the foxes disappear we will lose the countryside's main predator and soon be faced with a plague of rabbits, voles and mice. Equally serious is the threat to the badgers, who die being caught by mistake in the snares. Would my children, I wondered, grow up to know Brock the Badger and Charlie the Fox only as animals that, like the Teddy Bear, have no existence other than as cuddly toys, or figures in story books?

# Squirrel pie

Winter can seem a very long season on a livestock farm. You have animals to feed morning and night, pens to muck out, hay and straw to be carted from the barns to the pens and the stalls. Once the morning's round of these labours (chores is too light a word for the hauling of heavy bales of fodder or heavy buckets of water) is over, there seem only a few brief hours of daylight before, in mid-afternoon, you start the whole process again.

It seemed to me important, soon after I immersed myself in farming, to get out and away from this enclosed wintry life, if only for an occasional hour or two during the week. One place near Micklebury provided, I discovered, a marvellous means for drawing back from these immediate pressures. This was an old hilltop fort called the Camp. It rates only the skimpiest mention in the county guide books. Local farmers dismiss it as a piece of poor, banky land fit for nothing but pasture for a few sheep. The more generous-minded will concede it provides some handy cover for young pheasants and forms a good spot from which to watch the local hunt. Yet the Camp is a place which, even on the bleakest of winter days, never fails to lift my spirits.

From the narrow road at the foot of the hill, you clamber over the gateway through the overgrown hedge, and make your way up the steep escarpment which men carved out of the hillside with bone spades well over two thousand years ago. At the flattened, ten-acre top, above the steep, ancient defensive ditches, the grass is broad-leaved and coarse, grass that has never been crushed by tractor wheels, or torn apart by ploughs and harrows, but has been flattened over the centuries only by the nibbling of sheep and the tramp of men's feet. Men took refuge here with their wives and children, cattle and sheep, to fight off other iron-age tribes in search of land and food. Later it served as a fortress against the Romans as they thrust towards Wales. To the people of those times the Camp represented life and survival. Today, it always conveys to me a sense of hope. Even in February there are signs that life is stirring again in the countryside. Amongst the brown, decaying fronds of bracken, the skeletal outlines of dead thistles, and the sodden and lifeless grass, hang the tiny tassels of purple catkins. A newly-trimmed hedge in the fields below glimmers with a faint green, as rising sap begins to colour the ends of the cropped twigs. The quilt of small, neat fields spread out in the valley below, mostly pale yellow and brown, will be broken by the vivid green of a field of winter wheat or barley, and you can sense the spring, distant though it may be.

I managed only one visit to the Camp that winter. Most of my life was conducted at a more prosaic level. It was a steady round of feeding the new baby, helping Tom to muck out horses and calves, feeding the baby, cooking meals, feeding dogs and chickens, feeding the baby, painting window-ledges and papering walls ready for the following holiday season. Indeed, come to think of it there is a remarkable similarity between looking after guests in a house and looking after animals in a stable. The animals are less trouble to feed, but a great deal more trouble to clean up after. Meals for humans call for much more than dipping a bucket into a food bin and tipping the contents into a manger, but at least a round with the vacuum cleaner is a good deal simpler than the inescapable farmyard routine of forking out heavy straw muck from the floor of a cattle pen. But what both animals and humans need is constant attention—or, to be more exact, constant, unobtrusive attention. Tom gave this to all our stock, unceasingly. After each feed he would study them closely. Did they need worming? Or delousing? Was there one slightly smaller than the others which was being bullied and pushed away from the feeding trough? Was that one breathing heavily showing the first signs of pneumonia? Was one of the cows in season?

I had learnt from my first few months in the holiday trade that it paid to give the same attention to each new group of guests. Did they want company in the evenings? Did they want Tom or me to join them in the sitting room, to answer their questions about the farm or the area, or—more often—to listen to their tales of their own lives? There seems to be some compulsion on people on holiday to unburden themselves to comparative strangers about their personal or family problems. On the other hand there were others who wanted, above all, privacy, the chance to feel that our sitting room was theirs for the time being, their haven of peace in this strange world into which they had penetrated.

Then there was the problem of food, or rather the problem of fitting the food to the guests. We served good, plain food and could afford to vary it only a little. Yet to some guests, particularly the elderly, it was not plain enough. They wanted only a boiled egg for breakfast, not our usual farmhouse fry-up of sausages, eggs, bacon and tomatoes. But you had to seek out their preferences. It is astonishing how reluctant we still are as a nation to express an individual preference, to opt out from the norm. I made a mental note that, however pressed I might be, I must sort out these matters with each new group as they arrived.

We decided that for the coming season we would try to gather in at least a few guests early in the spring, even if the cattle had not yet been turned out. There would be a period of difficult overlapping, with the animals to feed and muck out as well as the guests to serve, but it could bring in more useful cash. So we set about advertising early in the year. When I came to send off the cheque with the draft of the advertisements I realised that there was no money in the bank to meet it, unless I pleaded with the bank manager for a bigger overdraft. But I had resolved that in every particular the farm holidays were going to pay their own way. So I did something I had never done in my life before, and which I hope I shall never be forced to do again. I borrowed the money which my children had been given as Christmas presents. It was only a few pounds, but it met the need. But I had a feeling of guilt until, with the payment from the first of our guests, I was able to repay it to the Post Office account we had ear-marked for them.

The winter days also gave us a chance to talk over with our friends our experiences in that first season of taking guests. We were not lacking in neighbourly advice for the future. One evening, when we were huddled round the Aga in the kitchen, talking to John Hopkins and his wife Sue, I explained that our central problem was the way food prices kept rising steadily throughout the season, but that we could not keep adjusting our prices correspondingly. We had to fix a price at the start of the season and keep to it.

John Hopkins was never short of ideas. "You should make more use of the cheap food that there is to hand, instead of buying all that costly stuff in the supermarkets. Pigeons and squirrels. Now there's good meat available for the taking."

I was prepared to have my leg pulled, as an accepted local custom, but the idea of squirrel food went beyond a joke. But with these smilingly enigmatic men of the March you could never be quite sure, so I probed further. "Are you having me on again, John?" I queried, carefully.

John looked appropriately indignant. "Of course not. Why I said to the taxman only the other day 'Have you ever eaten squirrel? Because by the time you've screwed every penny out of us to pay your VAT, that's all we'll have left to eat.' He went away looking real worried."

"Anyway, you could ask Art Wilson. You know, he does a bit of hedging and roofing in between his trips to the Social Security. He was down at the Berrys' last week giving them a hand with the hedging and he had his dinner with them. They were chewing away and Jos Berry says: 'Squirrel, 'e makes a tidy curry doan 'e?' Well, Art he stops chewing in mid mouthful and says 'Go on, this ain't squirrel?'

"Joss said: 'Right enough it is. The lad shot him yesterday. He gets 5p for the tail. I skinned 'im and the missus cooked 'im. Not a bad meat. Not as good as a rabbit mind, but then this doesn't cost you nothing.'"

John Hopkins continued. "Art was quite put off. Couldn't finish his dinner. Course it wasn't squirrel at all. They were having him on. It was turkey curry."

Poor Art's culinary adventures did not end there. That weekend he went over to the Hopkinses to help with some roofing. John went on:

"Our boy David offered him a piece of the cold pie we had for dinner the day before. When he'd finished it David told him he'd just eaten squirrel and rabbit pie. But Art didn't believe him. He came outside and said; 'Your lad's a rum one. Gave me a piece of pie and tried to have me on that it was made of squirrel and rabbit.'

"It was," I said. "Good, wasn't it?" Art Wilson didn't know what to do with himself. He just stood there not knowing whether to believe me or not. He took off his hat and scratched his head and stared at me and said. 'I don't know. I reckon you people in Micklebury are going barmy.'"

The next time I found myself alone with Sue Hopkins I set out to discover the truth behind her husband's stories. She confirmed that in fact squirrel meat is not only edible, but can be made really palatable. It can be fried with onions and mushrooms, with a bit of bacon to sharpen up the taste, or be made the basis of a stew. Hereford cider, stirred into the stew as it is on the stove, is excellent at giving the meat a fuller taste. It sounded tasty enough, but I have never yet had quite enough nerve to try it on my own family, let alone on the fish-finger fixated guests.

Spring, as always nowadays, seemed again that year to be a long time coming. But my advertisement worked, and February and March brought us a cheeringly steady trickle of letters enquiring about holiday bookings, a most practical reminder that summer really was scheduled to start in three or four months' time. In fact we opened up to visitors far earlier than I had planned. On a black and windy night in early February the phone rang in the draughty passage between the kitchen and dining room. A couple who had stayed with us the previous season wanted to come back as early as possible.

"Are you open for Easter?" they asked.

"Easter? Oh, er, yes." I tried to keep the uncertainty out of my voice. I had no idea when Easter was. "Yes, that's fine. The last week of March. For two." I decided to add ten per cent to the rate we had charged the previous year. What a lovely business, I thought, where you can actually put up your price to keep pace with inflation. What a difference from our fate as farmers over the past three years, forced to accept a price for our cattle that never kept pace with inflation.

As I replaced the receiver, my elation at the prospect of opening at the end of March 'by popular demand', was replaced by a heavy sensation of doubt mainly centred in the pit of my stomach. Were we completely mad taking holidaymakers at a time of year when the road could well be partially submerged? Mad to take guests whilst I had a three-month-old baby still being breast fed? And mad to take guests when we still had all the stock in the barns, and so had the winter chores of feeding and mucking them out?

In the event, Easter week was not as chaotic as I had feared. The guests at least knew what they were coming to, knew us and above all knew our road. We were able to use their visit as a trial run to solve some of the problems we were bound to face in the summer. Not the least of our difficulties was that our lusty baby, William, woke noisily for his feeds at approximately ten p.m., two a.m. and six a.m. The last thing people want on holiday is their sleep shattered by a hungry baby, so we had to get him out of earshot. In the end we decided to move him into the attic bedroom above the kitchen, a cosy room that had once housed our succession of girl grooms. The kitchen below had been a later addition to the main house, built in 1908 in the true Herefordshire tradition. It was constructed of red engineering bricks that had once formed a wall running down one side of the lane. These had been brought up to the house to line a new well which was to be sunk. But the well was left unsunk and the bricks used for the kitchen instead. The kitchen was a fine big room and the area above had been listed as two extra bedrooms. In practice this meant one bedroom and one stairhead room. They were small but ideal for our needs. A separate staircase from the kitchen led up to them and they were insulated from the rest of the house by a two-foot stone wall. The only snag was that if this cut off the baby's cries from the guests, it also cut them off from me. So I moved into the 'annexe' with him. Tom decided to stay where he was and get some sleep for a change—or so he thought.

Meal times were the worst periods. The kitchen was like a mad house. Anthony had taken over the floor for his toy farm and when I was not being reprimanded for trampling in his hay field I was stepping on farm machinery constructed from sticklebricks. (Nothing, except a three-point plug, is more painful for the stockinged feet than a sticklebrick.) For Anthony, mealtimes coincided with maintenance sessions on his farm and he insisted I help repair his machinery. Two-year-olds, I learnt, are impossible to reason with when under pressure. The baby clearly did not intend to be outdone by his brother and sharp on the dot of the guests' meal times of nine a.m. and six p.m., he gave his lungs a thorough airing. Luckily there are three thick hardwood doors between our kitchen and living room, which when closed, stop the noise from the kitchen disturbing the rest of the household.

To fit the cooking in with the baby's feeds, I started to prepare the evening meal straight after our lunch. That is not as awful as it sounds, for we did not go in for such British culinary specialities as pre-roasted meat reheated by the application of boiling gravy. Nor did we dish up vegetables that had been reduced to a sodden mash by an afternoon in the bain marie (although there were times when I thought such fare would appeal to some of our more difficult guests). I prepared the vegetables in advance—peeling potatoes and cutting and washing fresh vegetables from the garden. And all the puddings were cold ones, or were pies or flans that can be cooked and heated up again without any detrimental effects.

I coped with the housework by carrying William with me in a baby sling, as I vacuumed, dusted and polished. Advertisements for baby slings claim that a mother can move around freely with baby carried comfortably in the sling. Perhaps the models photographed doing this were built on different lines to me, but I found that for all the muscular strength I had gained from five years' farming, twenty minutes of William in the sling was my limit. After that my shoulders and back would begin to ache painfully. Often I just had to keep going, particularly when dealing with the evening meal. Dinner, at 6 p.m., invariably clashed with feed time or post feed wind-up time. Either way I had a fractious baby on my hands who needed my full attention. I learnt to cook and wash up with William in the baby sling. Carving the meat with him slung round me proved however to be impossible, as did serving at table. I coped with that by parking him in his pram outside the kitchen window in the lean-to where we stored the firewood, within sight but out of earshot.

However, the main problems were not caused by the baby, but by his two-year-old brother. Perhaps we should have foreseen this. Anthony's world had been turned upside down within the space of a few months: first there was another child in the family who took most of his mother's attention, then complete strangers appeared in the house, strangers who took over the living room and yet did not live as members of the family, as did friends and relations who stayed with us. Finally his mother had moved out to a remote part of the house with the small intruder. The outcome was that Anthony started to yell in his sleep.

To calm him, Tom moved into the spare bed in Anthony's room. That produced quiet, but only until five in the morning. At that time Anthony started to get up and to make his way through the house. Occasionally one of the three hardwood doors would be closed against him. His frantic banging on the door and yelling for it to be opened, woke the household. He dogged my footsteps, following me everywhere. The farm on the kitchen floor spread and he took over most of the large, wooden kitchen table like an animal desperately establishing its territory. I felt sadly guilty at the way the farm holiday enterprise was upsetting my small son.

We had no ewes producing cuddly lambs as an Easter attraction but Angel's daughter, Bambi, had a strong black Aberdeen Angus bull calf on Easter Monday. Tom soon named him Buffy, which sounds the sort of nickname that nannies give their aristocratic charges, but referred to the little calf's habit of buffing Tom whenever he went near him. Buffy's appearance trenchantly affirmed his parentage. He was a cross between an Aberdeen Angus and a Limousin/Jersey; between a small dark Scot (the brown equivalent of the violent variety to be seen digging up the turf at Wembley) and a persistent continental Romeo. He formed a strong attachment to Tom, who in turn grew to hate him. As Buffy grew older he would rush at Tom when he entered the pen at feeding times, nuzzling his legs with the lolling affection of a simpleton. When Tom shook up the litter straw Buffy was so enthusiastic in his attentions that Tom could hardly keep hold of the pitchfork. I could afford to laugh at his antics: Buffy was not at all friendly towards me. If I helped Tom with the jobs he would approach me suspiciously, sniff and saunter off.

At least his mother doted on him. After he was born, Bambi would lick him from head to toe for hours on end. After a couple of days we had to shut him away from her in another box because this meant that he was never dry and we feared he would catch pneumonia. In all other respects, though, Bambi proved to be an excellent cow. She was soon yielding six gallons of milk a day, so Tom went into market and bought another three small calves for her to rear. We were particularly interested in her success because of her breeding. As a Limousin crossed with a Jersey, she would, we hoped, add hardiness and size to the traditional Jersey milking qualities. The idea of crossing Britain's lighter dairy breeds with continental species is now gaining ground, but in those days the 'exotics', as the European imports were termed by sceptical farmers, were regarded with extreme suspicion.

We were now firmly a two-cow family. Bambi was such a success (except for a phobia about little Anthony, whom she attacked at every opportunity) that the memory of our previous attempt at cow-keeping was blotted out. We decided therefore to keep Angel's new calf, a delightful heifer called Honey, and put her in turn in calf that autumn. Eventually we hoped to become a four-cow family.

Despite all these stresses, the week with our Easter guests went well and after they had gone we had a breather for several weeks. The previous year a few people had wanted to come for early holidays and I expected to get one or two April bookings. But that year people seemed to have realised, as T.S. Eliot says, that 'April is a horrid month.' They were no longer to be lured away from their cosy hearths by evocative tourist-board advertisements showing young lovers sitting amongst the daffodils or baby lambs gambolling under budding trees. Most people believed, quite correctly, that in a cold, wet April the English countryside can be decidedly unattractive.

Out on our cold, sodden pastures the crows were back, numerous and arrogant, strutting up and down under the black, naked trees. Jackdaws took up residence on top of both our main chimneys, dropping sticks, hay, dried manure and shreds of tissue paper into our bedroom. We began a sustained campaign to evict them from the living-room chimney, with brushes from below and cartridges from above. Feathers flew and furious squawks resonated down the chimney, but the jackdaws steadfastly refused to move on. Eventually we conceded defeat to the black devils and stopped lighting the fire.

In the end we did get one booking in April—one couple for one night. To celebrate the occasion we gave them the full red-carpet treatment, or to be more accurate, the electric-blanket treatment. I turned on all the electric storage heaters and dished up steak and chips followed by cherry cheesecake.

Once again we feared William might yell the house down in the middle of the night—not an occurrence calculated to encourage trade—so he and I went into exile in the bedroom above the kitchen.

"You never know," I said to Tom, "they might stop here on their return journey or come back next year or even recommend us to friends."

Though the bedroom above the kitchen was directly over the Aga, it was far from warm. It was indeed the coldest room in the house. When I climbed the narrow stairs late that evening it was even colder than it had been at Easter. I was slightly puzzled too by a faint, lingering smell. Tom brought me a cup of tea before going to our comfortable bed in the main part of the house. I mentioned the whiff to him.

"I must be going mad, but I swear I can smell town gas."

Tom stuck his nose in the air and did an olfactory search of the room.

"Yes, I think I can smell something. Probably a dead rat under the floorboards, or perhaps a dead bird in the roof space."

I accepted his explanation with a nod. Such hazards are a normal concomitant of farm life. Sound sleep was another concomitant of life on the land. But not that night. At half-past midnight William woke up and screamed his head off. Surprisingly he did not seem hungry so I cuddled him and gave my particularly tuneless version of 'Rock A–Bye Baby' until he went back to sleep. He woke again two hours later, looking very pale and crying more loudly than he had done in his life. My own head throbbed agonisingly. "Oh no," I thought wearily, "now he's teething." I fed him and eventually managed to settle him down. At six he woke again. My head was now exploding with pain. I fed the baby and crept downstairs. With a shaking hand I filled a glass with water and swallowed two aspirins and then lay on the sofa to summon enough strength to get to my feet. After half an hour I was appallingly sick. The thought of cooking a fried farmhouse breakfast for the guests and organising the children's breakfast made my head spin and my stomach turn over again. I crawled up to our bedroom and woke Tom up.

"William's been awake half the night and I feel as sick as a dog. You'll have to do the guests' breakfast." Then something in my fogged, fuddled brain clicked.

"Oh, my God! We've been gassed. That smell last night. The Aga fumes must be blowing back into the bedroom. Hell, we'd better get Willy out of there."

On the other side of the house we found William sleeping deeply—too deeply. As I gathered him into my arms I was alarmed to see his normally pink cheeks had acquired a distinctly green tinge. We rushed him downstairs and into the fresh air and took it in turns to carry him round the farmyard. After a minute or two he woke up, started to shriek and was then sick. I glanced up at the grey slate roof of the farmhouse. The jackdaws were no longer sitting on the living-room chimney. My eyes travelled along the roof. They had a new home. They were busy putting the finishing touches to a nest on top of the kitchen Aga chimney, a nest with under-floor heating provided by the Aga fumes which were being diverted into the bedroom below. Tom fetched his gun from the house and fired a couple of cartridges at them. He missed the jackdaws, but they took off in a flurry of squawks, never to return. Perhaps they were as weary of us as we were of them.

The immediate crisis was over. William's brain did not appear to be addled although he was making no secret of the fact that he had a severe headache. But nothing holds up the work on a farm. Come what may, animals have to be looked after. Tom strode off towards the feed shed.

I went shakily back into the kitchen and strapped wailing William into his chair. I tried to switch my mind off and pretend I wasn't there, pretend I was someone else as I dressed Anthony and cooked the guests' breakfast. I prepared my mind for the next task—facing up to guests whose night must surely have been ruined. Yet as I went through the doorway that separated our living quarters from the guests, it was like stepping through a looking glass into a different world. The toy strewn bedlam in the kitchen suddenly ceased to exist for me. I was back in a normal tidy world where people did not get gassed because intransigent jackdaws sat on chimneys.

I tried hard to smile. "Good morning. Did you sleep well? I hope you were warm enough. It's still a bit nippy for late April isn't it?"

The guests beamed back. "Yes, thank you. We slept like logs. It's a very comfortable bed, and it's so nice to be away in the quiet, with no traffic noise."

When I had served up the bacon and eggs, I walked round the yard again with the baby. By the time the guests appeared in the kitchen to pay their bill, he had calmed down a little. The visitors paused to make baby noises to him.

"Cooche-ee coo. Oocheee-coochee-coo. Is he teething, poor love?" asked the wife sympathetically.

I nodded numbly. I could hardly admit he was recovering from a dose of carbon monoxide and sulphur dioxide.

It was the first of a series of extraordinary calamities that season.

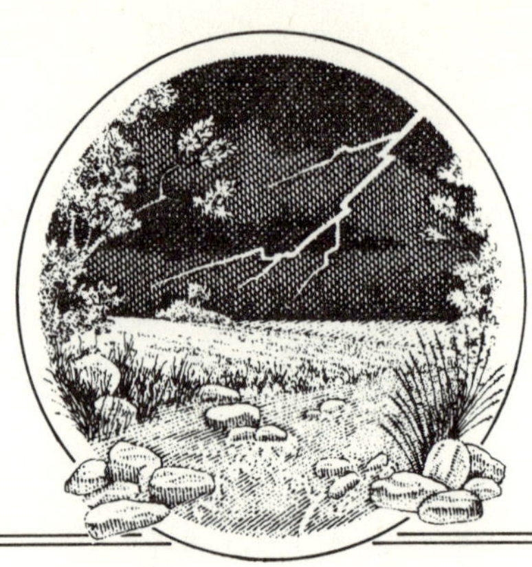

# Runaway road

My early advertising drive may not have brought any real flow of guests in April, but it had produced good bookings for May and a promising number of firm bids for later months. But it was clear that May Day, when the Prices were due to come back for their second visit, would be the true opening to our guest-house season.

It should have been, too, the opening for us of our spring farming season, when the cattle and horses were at last released from the barns and stables and when we, too, were released from our winter bondage of housing and feeding them indoors. In the days of warmer springs, the first of May was the traditional date for 'turning out', the date by which the grass was long enough and strong enough to provide good nourishment and to stand up against the impact of hooves. Turning Out day had established itself as a very red letter day in our farming calendar, a moment to savour.

As we opened the farm gate, we would watch the cattle speed off, galloping, kicking, bucking, leaping and racing round the boundary hedges. We hoped we had plugged all the gaps that had appeared in the hedgerows during the winter, because if the cattle found any weak spots on their preliminary gallop they would be in the next county before we could release our collie, Lyn, to round them up. They had a ritual of racing round once, twice, sometimes three times, and then of setting about establishing the herd's social order. Cattle from different pens would engage in trials of strength, butting, pushing, shoving. The victors would be the leaders—the chosen few who decided when the herd would file up to the trough or pond for a drink, and which area of pasture would be grazed at particular times of the day.

We were quite as full of joy and relief at their release as they were. Their freedom was our liberation from the winter chores of feeding and mucking out. That was all over for another five months. As long as the sun shone, the rain fell and the grass kept growing, the cattle could more or less look after themselves. For our part, we could concentrate on gathering in forage for next winter. Life was good.

But May Days of late have not been like that any more. Perhaps it was tempting fate to institutionalise the day by turning it into a Bank Holiday. Now they seem to be cold or wet or both. This year was no exception and as April drew to a close there was no real sign of spring weather. The air was unseasonably silent; the birds' spring chorus was muted; there were no bees and no cherry blossom, not even any hawthorn blossom. All around us the woods and copses were still black and bare; hedgerows that normally burst into leaf in mid-March showed no hint of green. I managed to mow the lawn and remove the sheet of polythene pinned over the front door and brought out our new sign—REGISTERED WITH THE ENGLISH TOURIST BOARD. It was my pride and joy.

"Show's we're doing the job properly," I announced proudly to anyone and everyone within earshot.

The Prices were with us early on May Day afternoon. Tom and I regarded their return visit as an auspicious sign. They were astonished to see William. Mrs. Price gasped. "Good heavens. So you dropped one in the off season."

But the weather remained dour. In the early evening Tom and I huddled into our parkas and trudged over the wet, spongy pastures to assess the rate at which the grass was growing, and to estimate when we could turn out the cattle. Up by the pond the grass was so short it could have been a golfing green; it had not grown at all since the previous autumn. Thick dark mist clamped down over the countryside, chilling and wet.

"We'll have to make less hay this year," Tom decided. "We must turn out the cattle during the day, at least, next week because we're almost out of barley. They'll have to go on one of the hay grounds. It's the only answer."

We walked slowly back to the farmhouse. There are no victories in man's battles with the elements, only truces and defeats.

But the weather did not dismay the Prices. They seemed to enjoy their week fully, and promised once again to return the following year. And no sooner had they gone than true spring was on the way to greet our next guests. The skies began to clear, the thick clouds collapsed into thin air and a hazy sun blinked uncertainly through the mist. Up the drive chugged two elderly but cherished cars. The leader, a Morris Minor with a split windscreen, was a type which went out of production around 1957. I had not seen one since my childhood. From the cars emerged our next guests, the Charltons and the Whittackers. They were four pensioners who were having their first holiday for years. They were members of a concert group that gave performances in old people's homes—mostly to audiences several years younger than themselves. They radiated an instinctive cheerfulness. In the evenings they sat in the lounge singing all the old songs—'Lily of Laguna', 'The More We are Together', 'Danny Boy'.

I loved catering for people who were enjoying them-selves. Anthony adored them as well and soon became Deerpark's equivalent to a Butlin's Redcoat. In the mornings when I went into the lounge to serve breakfast he would race in front of me, throw open the door and roar: "Good Morning, guests." They would roar back: "Good Morning, Anthony." When his father greeted him in the same manner he would object angrily: "I only say 'Good Morning' to the guests."

The Charltons and the Whittackers were perhaps too kind to Anthony and this was to cause trouble later on. They brought him chocolate every day and sometimes other presents. He began to expect sweets from people, and indeed became quite cunning at canvassing for presents. He would select a likely victim and when I was out of the way, raise the subject by the simple method of asking: "Have you got a present for me?" One guest jokingly commented on this to Tom, who told Anthony, "You mustn't ask everyone for presents". Anthony was deeply offended. "Dad, I don't ask everyone for presents. I only ask the guests."

I found that other families who offered accommoda-tion faced the same problem. The four-year-old daughter of a bed and breakfast landlady in Leominster used to tell the guests that it was her birthday—a statement which was often worth a pound note.

It was while the Charltons and the Whittackers were with us that we faced the first of many clashes that year between the needs of the farm and the needs of the guest house. This clash centred on the delicate subject of the duties of the stallion which had joined the ranks of our animals the previous autumn. We planned to save the expense of stud fees for the mares by serving them with our own colt, who was descended from a Derby winner. The only snag in this plan was that the colt was young and headstrong and the younger mare was not yet broken in. They were remarkably inexperienced in the equine facts of life. The mare, when faced with the stallion, tended to move off with an amazing sideways gallop and drag the hapless assistant stud groom (me) along for a run at the end of the halter rope. To prevent both stallion and mare disappearing down the farm road to Micklebury we were forced, in the earlier part of the season anyway, to serve the mares in an enclosed space. The only suitable enclosed space was the farmyard. But that was overlooked by the house and so by the guests.

Normally we had the stallion serve the mares while the guests were out for the day. But this was not always possible. On the Wednesday of the week the Charltons and Whittackers were at Deerpark, we were just about to start work with the horses when our four guests arrived back for an early tea. I was just about to take the tray in when Tom put his head round the kitchen door.

"Ask them if they would mind moving their cars into the stackyard for twenty minutes. We don't want any damaged paintwork."

"You must be joking," I exploded. "I'm not going into the lounge where they are all waiting for tea and ask them to move their cars because we are about to serve some mares. What will they think?"

Tom sighed. "I'll go and ask them, then. Those mares must be served today. This is a farm. We can't hold up the work because the guests might be offended."

The guests had seen too much of human nature, if not of animal nature, to be surprised. They complied willingly with Tom's request. Far from being offended they appeared on the yard with cameras. Being a true townie at heart I was horribly embarrassed. The following day Mr. Charlton approached me at teatime jauntily jangling his car keys.

"Shall I move my car?" he asked hopefully.

"No thanks," I replied with relief. "They've all been seen to today."

Disappointment swept over his face. "We'll be doing them again tomorrow evening," I added. He did not miss that occasion. He recorded it on cine film.

We realised, however, that we would have to organise the stud work differently. We could not serve the mares when children were around—and parents with young children often hung around the farm all day. There was only one interval when their eyes were not on the farmyard. That was at meal times. So if the need arose when we had families staying, I would serve the soup and the meat course, rush out of the house and hold a mare and then race back to the kitchen, wash my hands and serve the pudding.

Luckily we did not have to go through that Whitehall farce routine when the Whittackers and the Charltons were with us. They were ideal guests, always cheerful and always cheering us up. On their tours round the countryside they sang their concert songs and stopped by the roadside to brew up elevenses and tea on a primus stove. All four of us were sad to see them leave, for even Willy fell silent when they were in full song.

Life was far from enchanting the following week. Our next visitors, a pleasant elderly couple called the Roberts, brought me face to face with one of the biggest drawbacks of taking visitors, a drawback worsened when there is only one bathroom. That drawback is other people's stomach troubles, which rapidly become your own family's stomach troubles. The sight of a bottle of kaolin and morphine mixture in their room warned me, and I rushed about planting nail brushes and bottles of Dettol next to the wash basin and the kitchen sink. I scrubbed my hands till they were bare and washed all the Roberts' crockery and cutlery separately from ours. I boiled the tea towels. From the precautions I took, the poor Roberts could have been suffering from smallpox rather than gastro-enteritis. But it made no difference. Anthony, William and I all went down with the bug. Life was complicated still further because the Roberts seemed to have taken up residence in the bathroom. The week became a nightmare. Tom managed to stay clear of the germs and helped me as much as he could, but he too had the farm to manage single-handed. By Friday, after four nights with only a few hours of broken sleep, I was fit for the local asylum. I knew I could not cope with the next lot of guests due to arrive on Saturday. But fate came to my aid. On Friday evening the phone rang. The visitors we expected the next day could not make it. There had been a death in their family. They apologised profusely and insisted on paying the full amount. I offered them another holiday at the end of the season and put the phone down hardly able to believe my luck. I was to have a week's holiday—and a paid holiday at that.

Now I had the chance to enjoy Deerpark's surroundings. For the first time in the four and a half years that Tom and I had lived there we took our ease. The non-existent spring had given way to early summer. I lay on the grass in our tiny garden in the warm, reviving sunshine, or played with William in the shade of the porch. It grew hotter and I fulfilled my ambition to swim in the dewpond, which had at least two feet of brown, gluey water in it. I had forgotten the delights of slowly propelling myself through silty pond-water, drifting from a cool spot to an unexpectedly warm one. After a few days Tom swore the pool was full of leeches. I did not believe him for a minute . . . and yet. The possibility spoilt the Elysian delights for me. I never felt like swimming in the pond again after that May.

All too soon it was Whitsun Bank Holiday weekend and other people's holidays were back with us. At least it was the best Whitsun for years. A blazing white sun beat down out of a metallic-blue sky. Cattle lazed under the old trees, nodding their heads steadily in an effort to throw off the magnetic clouds of flies. Trees, in their first fresh glory of full leaf, brought the green back to a skyline that had for so many months been etched with the outstretched arms of bare trees.

Our guests for the week, parents, son and daughter-in-law all called Simpson, were late. And that presented a problem because with a young baby I had to stick to a fairly rigid timetable to get everything done. I was in a quandary. Should I start feeding the baby? Tom was out, so if the guests arrived in the middle I would have to cover myself up quickly and try to stem his screams of deprivation. I decided to feed him. I sat by the window of the bedroom as I did so and kept a watchful eye out for the guests. By the time William was finished the winding farm track, white and dusty now in the hot, evening sunlight, was still empty. I sat there for some time nursing the baby. Then I saw two figures walking up the road. As they came nearer I could see they were two women, one of whom was leaning heavily on a stick. In trepidation I ran down to meet them.

"Our car's broken down," the younger woman gasped. "We hit something on your road. Can you give us a tow?"

My heart thudded. The road had to claim a victim sooner or later. That wretched track. I had put twenty tons of stone into the holes at the beginning of the season. Would it ever stop coming to bits?

Action was needed. I wished Tom was at home. The two women, Mrs. Simpson senior and Mrs. Simpson junior were clearly very weary. At the same time their husbands were stranded down by our neighbour's barn, after a five-hour journey in Bank Holiday traffic. And I could not leave William on his own, anyway. Tea, as always, seemed to be the answer. I made a full strong pot of it. Mrs. Simpson took charge of William while I roared off down the road in our car. To my immense relief—when I towed vehicles I tended to jerk bits off them—I met Tom in the lorry coming up the road. With him were the Simpson menfolk and their luggage. The road, Tom was quick to tell me, was not to blame after all. The Simpsons' car had simply overheated on the long journey in the traffic.

More cups of tea and the substantial evening meal helped the Simpson party to calm down, although I was not sure they were completely convinced that their car was not a victim of our farm road.

They were a family who had clearly recently been under strain. From them I was to learn another point about farm holidays. The Simpsons had been recommended to take a quiet, restful holiday, and had opted for one on a farm as answering this prescription. Other farmers' wives had had similar guests, who had chosen a farm holiday as the cheaper—indeed much cheaper—equivalent of an ocean cruise. Sometimes I thought there must be doctors throughout Britain advising their patients:

"You need a holiday. Somewhere quiet and away from crowds. What about staying on a farm?"

If this is so, it is a risky prescription. Though farms are free from traffic noise, and if well-situated, as Deerpark certainly is, you have beauty right on your doorstep. But farms are also places of work, with the pressures and strains of activity all around you. They tend to be isolated, so that you are denied that quiet stroll to the shops, that chance to potter amidst crowds which can be one of the most restful of all activities. And to this, we at Deerpark could add the daily hazard of the drive up our road, which required, to say the least, good concentration.

The road became a matter uppermost in the Simpsons' minds. They worried greatly about the repairs to the car, and worried even more that, once repaired, it might not stand up to the road. When they got it back from the garage, they nursed it up the roadway with constant care. I found myself beginning to worry too, about the way their holiday seemed to offer them strain more than rest. The only suggestion I could make was that they took more walks on the farm and guided them on my own favourite routes around the coppice and to the dewpond. I was helped in this because the weather at last grew hot—in fact, too hot. There had been no rain for three weeks—a critical deprivation at that time of year. Before our eyes the grass became dusty and tired as it stopped growing. Around the five pine trees by the front gate— groups of five pines were regarded locally as Capability Brown's signature on his work—the turf was burnt and dead where the soil lay thinly over the shallow Herefordshire sandstone. The scene had too many echoes of 1976 to be pleasant. That year had taught us that drought was no longer a climatic phenomenon that brought havoc only to faraway places in the American West, Bengal and Upper Volta. We were wary now of dry weather, and longed for the rain we had cursed a month earlier.

Our drought scare was a false alarm. A couple of days later the radio was forecasting occasional and scattered showers. By mid-afternoon, black clouds loomed up from the south. The eerie stillness that precedes wild and reckless summer storms settled slowly on the surrounding countryside. The world seemed to hold its breath. In the distance we could hear the soft rumble of thunder. But we doubted whether we would be lucky enough to receive one of the occasional storms. To increase our chances I performed a rain dance on the lawn with Anthony. William bounced up and down in his chair until he had manoeuvred it into the feathery nigella which he then proceeded to tear to pieces with great glee.

Later, as I was preparing our evening meal, the rain

came—two outbursts of twenty minutes of heavy, thudding drops of water. A river of water cascaded off the fields and over the farmyard. Half an hour later the dry, parched ground had absorbed every drop. A faint evening breeze even whipped up a small dust storm from the dried-out earth.

But that was only a foretaste. Perhaps we should not have mocked the forces of nature with our rain dance on the lawn. The following day the rain came with a vengeance. Perhaps I was also tempting fate by making a rare trip to the hairdresser in town. When I entered the hairdresser's it was a bright, sunny summer day. When I left it an hour later, I stepped into the half-light of a nightmare world. A false dusk was spreading menacingly towards the town from the south. There was a sudden chill in the air. For a moment I had the feeling that the sensation of doom that overhangs the Marches on some days was materialising in a more visible form. It was easy to believe that forces of darkness were closing in on us.

A jagged thrust of lightning ripped the sky, and the heavens boomed with thunder. The sky seemed to collapse on the town. What came down on us cannot be described as rain—that is delivered in drops. This was a solid sheet of water.

Within five minutes the roads flowed like rivers. Street drains, overwhelmed with water, spouted the rain back again, shooting it three feet into the air like fountains. I fought my way to the car hanging on to the street signs to keep my balance against the wall of water. In the car I was safe—so long as I stayed put. But I had to get back to Deerpark to cook the guests' evening meal. I could hardly see out of the windows and the windscreen wipers made little difference; it was like driving through a waterfall. As I crept along through the foot of fast flowing water that only an hour before had been the A.49, I could see cars halted along the length of the verge as drivers decided not to risk driving in the treacherous conditions. I felt light-headed with relief when I reached the turning for Micklebury and when half a mile further on I reached the turning into our lane. But the lane was not there any more. Instead a foaming torrent poured out of the cut between the trees—a tumbling, rushing rapid of water, bricks, mud, stone. There was no hope of driving the car up it, so I stopped and waited for the storm to pass. After five minutes John Hopkins drew up beside me in his car. He offered shelter and a cup of tea in his farmhouse, so we drove to his farm in a slow convoy through the rising flood water.

Watching the rain lashing the walls and streaming down the windows I wondered where it all came from. Never had I seen such rain. After about an hour the storm seemed to be wearing itself out and finally after another half-hour the rain stopped. We set out to see if it was possible to reach Deerpark. By then it was after six o'clock and I wondered what had happened to the Simpsons. Along the road the flood water was two feet deep in places. John found it exhilarating.

"I love driving around after a storm looking at the damage. You want to go round Upper Hill in April—it's very banky up there and after a good soaking there are rows upon rows of potatoes washed up on the road."

I nodded in agreement. I knew what he was getting at. The full force of Nature's wrath, particularly in the normally tranquil English countryside, can present an awesome spectacle. At the same time farmers derive considerable solace from the sight of other farmers' misfortunes. It was highly likely that the following day local farmers viewing their washed out sugar beet or potatoes would say to each other:

"Look at they people at Deerpark over Micklebury way. They got no road now. All three quarters of a mile of it's gorne. Just like that. Cost them just a tidy sum to repair it."

We reached the Fox and Pheasant and on the topside of the slope of the car park, like a huge piece of jetsam thrown up by the flood waters, was the Simpson's car.

They were standing by it, looking excited and cheerful, their own tensions swept aside in facing the storm. This sudden need to face an emergency had clearly done them far more good, given them a far better break from their own problems, than any period of rest. There was a lesson there somewhere, I told myself. Talking eagerly, they went into the pub for a drink and I promised to ring them to report on the state of the road, if and when I reached Deerpark.

It seemed as if the continuous rural battle against the elements had involved everyone, kindling a Dunkirk spirit and diminishing less tangible problems.

I headed the car gingerly up the lane. The damage was severe. The exact extent of it was difficult to assess because water was still flowing fast over the surface. I could, however, feel bumps and deep holes that had not been present earlier in the afternoon. When I reached the house I noticed the nappies had been torn off the washing line and hammered into the cabbage patch. Tom thankfully thrust a screaming William into my arms and went back down the lane to act as a pathfinder in our car, to guide the Simpsons back to the farm. Just to complete the disaster, the electricity was off and I was faced with preparing a three-course meal on the Aga.

The following morning was clear and sunny. The road was a devastated mess. Hundreds of tons of stone had been swept off it by the water and carried down into the village. Much of it had ended up in the garden of some luckless council tenants. They had recently moved into the house and had worked night and day to transform into a garden what had been a muddy patch by transplanting hundreds of plants from their former garden. (It is normal practice in Herefordshire to uproot most of the contents of the garden and take them with you when you move.) Now it looked like a small quarry. Our road had no central strip any more. In places, a two-foot gorge had been cut out of it by the force of the water.

Tom and I got out of the car at the top of the lane and looked sadly at the damage. We had surfaced the road ourselves, foot by foot. Although it was not an 'adopted' road the council had deemed it a footpath and had therefore supplied us with 300 tons of stone so that we could make it up ourselves.

The half-dozen households who used the road got together with children, uncles, cousins—any who could use a shovel—to lay the stone as the council lorries tipped it. Shovelling and spreading stone is very hard labour. It took us two days, but at the end we had the satisfaction of seeing a road that was better than many of the council's own. Now you would need climbing boots to negotiate it on foot.

We had to do something about it and quickly, or our entire farm holiday business would be a washout in every sense of the word. Tom rang Sid Williams, a local earth-moving contractor. He was due to visit us to deepen the septic tank's outflow ditch. Sid agreed to come up that evening with his earth mover. In Herefordshire people always agree to do jobs when asked. To refuse would be rude. But such agreement does not necessarily mean they will in fact turn up. What if Sid does not come, I wondered? Should I phone next week's visitors and warn them? Perhaps they could park their car at the pub and we could ferry them up and down the road in our car, which, with its hydraulic suspension, managed the lane readily enough. Sid said he would be with us by six. When he had not arrived by then I fretted and fumed. At eight his wife phoned to say he was on his way. Tom went down the road to meet him. Fifteen minutes later he was back.

"Was it impossible?" Despair swept over me. Tom put a comforting arm round me.

"It's all right. Sid's done a beautiful job. He's graded out the stone that's left on the side of the lane and the surface is better than ever."

I could have cried with relief. But a more practical form of gratitude was required. I went into the kitchen to rustle up tea and doorstep ham sandwiches. Sid set to and dug out the septic-tank ditch. I do not know why the sight of a JCB taking great bites out of the earth is so riveting but the Simpsons came into the field and watched Sid at work with wide-eyed fascination. The smell was appalling. I wondered if our guests were aware of what Sid was doing. If so, they gave no sign. It was clear that the sight of Sid and his JCB in action was the high spot of their holiday.

They were in high spirits when next day, being Saturday, they packed to go. Their tension and strain had disappeared. The younger couple even vowed to return on their own one day. As their car started off down the road I could not resist a quick peek at the visitors' book before I tore round and changed all the beds ready for the new arrivals. I wondered what future guests would make of the Simpson's entry:

"Everything 100 per cent—even the rescue service."

# An educational rodeo

Tom was sure that once the mares were in foal they could be safely turned out with the stallion to grass in the front pasture, along with the cattle. Stallions do not normally force their attentions on mares in foal. Their technique is to gather their herd of mares into a corner of a field and, with head lowered, move up and down behind them rather like a sheepdog keeping sheep up together. In that way they can keep a check on whether any of the mares are coming into season. Our stallion was less subtle. His technique was to select one of the mares and then pursue her up and down the field at about thirty miles per hour. When the luckless female was completely exhausted the stallion would cover her whether she was in foal or not.

These frequent and often violent encounters did not worry Tom at first. "He'll settle. He's only young. He's got to learn his job."

I was less confident. "My God! That maniac is roaring up and down the field covering those mares at every opportunity. The guests are being treated to a continual sex show six yards from the lounge window. Horses aren't exactly discreet are they? I mean, they don't pick a quiet spot under a hedge. He keeps catching them by the farmyard gate, so you can hardly miss it."

Tom refused to budge. "I can't put him in another field

because all the other grounds are shut up for hay. And I can hardly keep the poor animal shut in a stable all summer just because of the guests."

A few days later he changed his mind. He agreed it might be wiser to shut the stallion in his stable because he might be hurt by one of the kicks the now exasperated mares were showering on him. Our problem was how to catch the stallion. He was so preoccupied with the mares that he merely tossed his head with indifference and trotted off when Tom approached with a bucket of oats. We were just discussing tactics when the older mare came galloping towards the farm gate with the stallion in hot pursuit. The answer was in front of our eyes. Tom opened the farmyard gate and both horses flashed by us, hooves flying and manes streaming. I tried to shoo them away from the guests' cars, a red Cortina belonging to one couple, the Lloyds, and a blue Allegro of their friends, the Barnets. Our 'CARS PARKED AT OWNERS' RISK' notice was unlikely to protect us from claims lodged as a result of damage inflicted by mating horses. But the mare and the stallion went straight past my outstretched arms and missed the cars by a hair's breadth. They pounded on, past the barn, past the stables and again past the guests' cars, and then began another circuit. The stallion's chestnut coat was lathered with sweat, his ears flattened, his nostrils flared and his eyes blazing with determination. Before him the brown mare fled with equal determination.

"Do something," I screamed at Tom. "They'll smash the cars up in a minute."

On the next circuit Tom managed to direct the two galloping horses away from the cars and they swerved down the concrete path by the stables towards the caravan. With a sudden flash of horror I caught sight of Anthony, who had come to investigate the excitement, toddling down the narrow passage between the caravan and the stables. Before there was even time to yell a warning the two horses had shot by him, one on either side. They then tore up the narrow gap between the Cortina and the Allegro. A full five minutes must have passed since the horses had raced into the yard—plenty of time to alert our guests to the spectacle. At the lounge window that overlooked the yard were three peering faces, Mr. and Mrs. Lloyd and Mr. Barnet. Outside, the two demented horses were still tearing round the yard. Then they changed course and thundered into the barn. Sounds of kicking hooves and furious neighs issued from the building. Then there was a loud crash and the manure spreader, which had been parked there for repairs, emerged through the door followed by the two horses. They clattered into the nearby cow shed. Tom slammed the door behind them as the stallion took the victor's honours.

Luckily neither horse was any the worse for the chase, and within ten minutes we had them each in separate stables. As we pushed home the bolts on the door, Mrs. Barnet, the only guest not to have witnessed the race, arrived back from her walk down to the post box in Micklebury. She was a quiet pleasant woman with a stern manner tempered by a quick warm twinkle in the eyes.

"You've just missed all the excitement," Tom told her and described the scene.

Mrs. Barnet was open-mouthed. When Tom had finished she gasped.

"What happened at the end? Did he have his way with her?"

Her husband, who was a very upright bank manager, and the Lloyds had obviously decided to make nothing of the incident. "Bit of a to–do, eh?" was all Mr. Lloyd said when I went to serve the dinner. But they left a cryptic comment in the visitors' book. "Friendly folk, fine food. Even 'educational' entertainment by Deerpark rodeo."

Our horses were not the only animals to force their

attentions on the guests. Our farm road, which had a gate across it, wound up over the main pasture where the cattle were grazing. Every day on the dot of five o'clock, when most guests returned to the farm from their day's outing, the cattle would stroll up to the gate and mill around it. When a car drew up they would obstinately stand their ground. Only determined shooing, hand clapping, hooting and engine revving, would make them shift. I noticed that old hands at farm holidays invariably carried a walking stick in the car to cope with such situations.

But the animals which defied all our efforts to control them were the moles. They appeared, or rather their earthworks appeared, in the middle of June during the last spell of sunshine we were to enjoy in what was to become a damp and dismal summer. Behind the house the Black Mountains were no longer a lack-lustre grey, but a strong vibrant purple, and the fields stretching to the skyline were green with grass and healthy young crops. Even the brown earth of the potato and sugar beet fields was sprinkled with the green seedling plants. Indeed all around us the countryside was making up for the long dead winter and the long cold spring. The great oaks and beeches were at last in full leaf; on the perimeter of the farm the dark forbidding woods were alive with birdsong and with the scuttling of small animals foraging for food to feed their growing young. Underfoot the harsh carpet of twigs and fallen leaves had been replaced by a mat of bluebell leaves and ground elder.

But by the house three brown ulcers of earth marred the smooth green surface of the lawn. When they first appeared I cleared the mound of earth away from the hole made by the mole and poked the soil back into the tunnel. There was hardly a sign of the mole's handiwork. Man had once again put the animal kingdom in its place, which is definitely outside the garden. Or had he?

The next day the bumps reappeared in exactly the same places and on the next day and the next and the next. The bumps became a constant reminder of the wayward force of nature that permeates the countryside. Try as we may, it is outside our control and has a nasty habit of asserting itself against our efforts to make our lives neat and tidy.

From the time these intransigent creatures arrived on the farm, nothing seemed to go according to plan. Bookings for the rest of the summer suddenly slackened off. After the third week of June we had only two more bookings for the whole of the rest of the summer. The fickleness of the holiday trade was puzzling. Bookings for the first part of the season had come in steadily; indeed we had been turning people away. Now it seemed that the world was going to end after June 17th, so few reservations did we have after that day. Why and when people booked holidays was a strange business. We would have no enquiries for weeks and then the phone would ring continuously for a couple of days. I was still advertising so I hoped we would get a rush of last-minute bookings.

In the event, we did not even have the house occupied until June 17th. The group that had booked the week, a party of four called the Bothwicks, came and went in less than a day. I had to be away from the farm for one night, so I left Tom, my mother and Anne Summers, a farmer's daughter from Micklebury, to hold the fort.

I left the farm before the Bothwicks had arrived, so the first I heard of the calamity was when I phoned Tom the following evening before catching the train home.

"They've gone," Tom told me in answer to my query about the state of things at Deerpark. "They left after breakfast."

"What do you mean?" I was aghast. I could hardly grasp the implication of what he was saying. "They booked in for the week. Some other people wanted that week too and I turned them away. I was counting on the Bothwicks to pay the coalman. We haven't anyone else coming until August."

"I'll tell you all about it when you get home." I could sense how exasperated he was.

Tom's account of what had happened made me feel hugely thankful that I had not been there to deal with the Bothwicks.

"They didn't get here until nine o'clock at night. We were waiting and waiting for them. Your mother and I didn't dare go and do anything else in case they arrived and no one was here to meet them."

"They were an oldish couple—mid-sixties—with a niece and her husband. They seemed all right, quite pleasant, although I didn't take to the old man. They said they liked the place. The old girl was leaning on her elbows looking out of the window, saying how beautiful it was and mooning over the horses. You know how these people go on: 'Ooh. Aren't they intelligent.'"

But the Bothwicks did not waste much time admiring their surroundings. Within half an hour they had piled into the car and shot off down the road to the Fox and Pheasant. They returned at midnight. Tom was alarmed. Hotels can cope with well-oiled guests, but they present a problem in what is, in fact, a private house, particularly when there are young children around. Tom hardly slept that night, disturbed at half-hourly intervals by the sound of old Mr. Bothwick labouring up and down the stairs, to and from the bathroom.

When Anne cleared away the dishes from the table the following morning she was taken aback to see four cold and untouched farmhouse breakfasts. Clearly something was amiss. Tom was not altogether surprised when a worried and apologetic Mrs. Bothwick junior poked her head round the kitchen door.

"I'm afraid we'll have to leave. I'm very sorry, but you see my uncle has a pacemaker in his heart, and he finds the stairs to the bathroom too much for him. We've paid a deposit, so that should cover the cost of the bed and breakfast."

I was puzzled. Downstairs bathrooms and lavatories are not uncommon. Tom explained. His estimate of the Bothwicks was that they had come not just for a country holiday, but for a country drinking holiday. A lot to drink makes an accessible lavatory highly desirable. And four hangovers would explain four untouched breakfasts of eggs, bacon, sausage and tomato.

I took heed of this incident and in future stressed to people, when they rang to make their bookings, that the bathroom and lavatory were downstairs. I then put my mind to increasing our sanitary arrangements. To put in a further loo upstairs was not practicable. We would have to resort to the techniques of our forebears. I decided I would invest in a couple of chamber pots. To my generation, their main use had been as arty-craft table ware, or as props in student rags. But not so long ago they were in common use in homes, hotels, university colleges and British Rail sleeping compartments.

I assumed that the present fashion for using chamber pots as salad bowls, punch bowls and flowerpot holders would mean I would have little difficulty in finding one or two for sale. This was not so. Our nearest market town has streets lined with antique shops that collect the everyday utensils of our heritage and ship them abroad in juggernaut lorries. As I went into one shop which had a container lorry parked outside with an NL plate on it, I pondered on the realities of the Common Market. The Dutch swamp the British market with beef produced far more expensively than in Britain, which they sell, with the aid of huge Common Market subsidies for less than our own homegrown meat. Then they move in with their lorries to buy up the furniture that we must sell to pay the bills. Somehow this did not seem to fit in with the idea of one big free-trade area we had been told the Market would bring.

That shop had no chamber pots on offer. These it seemed were now a rarity. Eventually I discovered two in one of the smartest local antique shops. The proprietor, who just to complicate matters, turned out to be Dutch, had so little use for them that he gave them to me for nothing, a gesture which mollified a little my anti Common Market sentiments.

That may have solved an immediate plumbing difficulty, but a solution to our major problem—the lack of bookings—was not so easily found. Yet we were perhaps fortunate not to have a full house that week because we were coming up once again to the dread rush of haymaking. We had decided this year to stagger our haymaking and so spread the risk of having the crop ruined by rain. We would cut only a few acres at a time. That week we cut our first five-acre patch. The weather immediately became wet and bitterly cold. As we had no guests and therefore no money, we could not afford to pay anybody to lug the bales into the barn for us. We had to do the job ourselves. I had forgotten how heavy a bale can be especially when you have already lifted 400 of them onto a trailer in an afternoon. I had forgotten too the added physical effort of stacking them in the barn, as the stack grows higher and the level of the bales on the trailer gets lower. A friend from the village declared that haymaking time was statistically the most popular time for farmers' wives to pack their bags and leave their husbands. I knew how they felt.

Just as we were giving up hope of ever seeing another paying guest, the telephone began to ring with more people making bookings. To my joy, one was for the following week from a couple who wanted to stay for ten days. The coalman would be paid sooner than we had anticipated.

The visitors, the Cartwrights, wanted to arrive the following Monday, a fact which did present a slight problem. We were due to be visited both by the man from the Ministry and by the vet.

In my advertisements I described Deerpark as a 'working farm'. No one, Tom and I agreed, could say that contravened the Trade Descriptions Act. But working farms have their detractions as well as their advantages. They are by their nature, messy. If we kept to a pattern by which guests arrived on Saturdays, I could make a special effort that day to tidy up the farmyard, and so let them get a good first impression, which would linger in their minds during the week as the farm was worked and a mess was made.

But that Monday we were particularly busy, as bureaucracy was arriving at the farm in force. Firstly we had to herd the cattle from the fields into the pens so the man from the Ministry of Agriculture could punch their ears to show they had received the calf subsidy. Then our local vet was due to come up and take blood samples from all our forty heifers for our annual brucellosis test.

For hour after hour we rushed around the pens, cornering the beasts one after another. Then we chased them one by one through the confines of the metal-barred cattle crush, which held them still while the vet took the blood samples. When by seven o'clock we had finished, the yard looked tatty and mucky, its grey gravel no longer raked in neat criss-crosses, but churned up with straw and dung.

Luckily for us the Cartwrights arrived late, so at least I had time to clean myself up and feed William. They were a couple in their mid-fifties who had retired early to the East Coast to look after Mr. Cartwright's crippled mother. Mr. Cartwright had a smooth friendly face, although his thin, compressed lips indicated that he might be a bit tetchy. His wife was large and what is politely termed portly and I watched anxiously as she mounted the stairs, but she negotiated them quite athletically.

Supper appeared to be a success and the Cartwrights complimented me on the lamb chops and lemon syllabub I had hurriedly prepared for them. Mr. Cartwright did seem slightly perturbed about the state of the road. But I had become so used to complaints about the road that I brushed his anxious questions aside with an impatient answer.

"It's fine really. The vet came zooming up here this afternoon in an MGB. Once you get used to it you hardly notice the bumps."

Tom and I spent a considerable time chatting to the Cartwrights that evening, because they were both compulsive talkers. When we managed to make our escape I remarked to Tom:

"That's a relief, anyway. They talk a bit, but they enjoyed the meal. I don't see them doing a bolt like the last lot."

I could not have been more wrong.

The following morning at breakfast, the Cartwrights seemed ill at ease. Soon afterwards there was a timid knock at the kitchen door. That disconcerted me for a start. Although I cleaned the kitchen about three times a day, it rarely stayed tidy for more than half an hour with Anthony and William on the job. At that time in the morning it looked like a rubbish tip. Anthony had lately taken to playing with cardboard boxes which were scattered about the floor in various stages in distintegration. Along with the boxes, the floor was, as usual, booby-trapped with sticklebricks; William had further embossed it with Weetabix thrown from his high chair. I was trying to clear this up when the knock came.

Mr. Cartwright put his head round the door and looked shocked at the mess. He was near to tears.

"My car's hurt," he said accusingly. "I think I've damaged my exhaust on your road. We went over a terrible bump last night and I heard something go."

I apologised profusely for our wretched road and followed him out to the yard.

To my relief Tom was outside tinkering with the blue tractor, and he looked up when he heard the kitchen door open. I caught his eye and motioned that he should join us.

"What's up?" he asked.

Mr. Cartwright's voice shook with agitation. "My car's exhaust has been injured on your road," he said.

"Let's have the bonnet up and listen to it," suggested Tom. Mr. Cartwright raised the bonnet with difficulty and then turned the ignition key. I almost expected the car to say 'arh', but it purred into life with the even, mechanical pulse that is symptomatic of a perfectly healthy engine. We peered into the gleaming entrails of the Marina.

"There's nothing wrong with the exhaust. There's no hint of blowing," diagnosed Tom.

Mr. Cartwright was not pacified. He wrung his hands with anguish.

"The engine doesn't sound right. We thought the bottom hit something on our way up yesterday. My wife and I went back down the road for a walk last night to see if there was anything we could have hit. There's a spot near the bottom which is very bad."

I had a sudden picture of the two Cartwrights shuffling down to the village and peering at the road in the gathering dusk. They must have thought the ramp, which diverted the water off the fields from the lower part of the lane, was the culprit.

Mr. Cartwright was saying petulantly. "Look underneath. You can see something has skinned the paint off the exhaust pipe there." Tom bent down to look. "There hasn't been any paint there for months. That's rust. The exhaust fumes always burn the paint off the pipe there."

"No, no. That's red oxide paint," argued Mr. Cartwright.

He switched the ignition on again and revved the engine.

"There. Can't you hear it's not right."

For the life of us, Tom and I could not hear anything wrong. Our ears are finely tuned to engine noises because when you drive a tractor on the land you must keep an ear cocked. You have to ensure that the machine is driven in the right gear and at the right speed for whatever job you are doing, on terrain that is constantly changing. However, Mr. Cartwright was convinced his car was in mortal danger and the disagreement was developing into an unpleasant wrangle. The customer is always right however mistaken he may be. I shook my head at Tom. "Don't argue. It won't do any good."

Mr. Cartwright put his hand in his back pocket and drew out his wallet.

"Look, if it's all the same to you, I'll settle with you now and we'll find somewhere else."

His words hit me like a blow in the face. Leave? They found Deerpark so awful they wanted to leave? It was the first time this had happened to me directly. The Bothwicks' departure had been cushioned for me by Tom. Even though the Bakers had warned us that we would get some guests who would want to leave, that it was something which happened to everyone in the holiday trade, when it did happen, it hurt. These were people who were not just spurning hotel accommodation. They were turning up their noses at my home. When I came to talk about this later to other farmers' wives who took paying guests, I realised that my reaction of anger and dismay was a common one. In due course, indeed, we accepted such occasional setbacks with a shrug of the shoulders. But that first occasion remains graven on my mind. Moreover, we needed the money.

At that moment there was not much I could do to improve the situation except be polite.

"If that's what you want it would be for the best."

I met Mrs. Cartwright on the stairs. She explained: "It's not the accommodation or the food. It's just the strain of the road. He couldn't take the strain of driving up and down it every day. The car was a retirement present and we'll never be able to afford another one."

"I'm very sorry. Don't let this spoil your holiday."

"Well, it is unfortunate. We've come all this way and now we've got to find somewhere else to stay. I don't see how we're going to find anywhere as reasonable as this."

As the Cartwright's car crept down the drive I sank into a chair in the kitchen. Tom made me a cup of coffee and tried to boost my morale. "There was nothing wrong with his car. But you get people who are hypocondriacs about their cars. They always think there is something wrong with them even when they are running perfectly. Remember what the Bakers told us before we went into this business. Everyone gets people who don't like the place."

I went over the Cartwrights' stay with us. "It's those damned modern British cars. I should have realised. The floors are so thin that you can hear the blades of grass in the centre of the road brushing the bottom of the car. They think that at any moment a jagged great rock will jump up and rip the bottom out of their car."

Were we mad, I wondered, trying to make money from paying guests with two small children and all these animals round our necks? The whole enterprise seemed to be coming apart before our eyes.

Did people really want holidays on farms? Or had the

boom years of 1975 and 1976 been due to the good weather and the fact that people had been unable to afford to go abroad? Perhaps the stay-at-home holidaymakers preferred guest-house accommodation with wash basins in the rooms and other facilities like games rooms and tennis courts. I looked back over the season so far—being gassed by the jackdaw that sat on the kitchen chimney; having the road washed away; being harassed by stomach bugs and by jumpy guests recovering from nervous breakdowns. Was it all worth it? We were certainly working very hard for every penny we made. I resolved that the moment livestock prices picked up I would never let another holidaymaker across the threshold.

As a diversion from these disappointments, I started a campaign to kill off the moles that were now indulging in widespread open-cast and subterranean mining on the front lawn. Mole smokes were the first weapon. They are things like fireworks which, when ignited, release not golden rain or green stars but dark clouds of noxious gasses. We bought three to start with and stuffed them down the largest runs. They certainly did their stuff. Smoke and poisonous gasses rose out of the grass as though the garden was about to heave upwards in a volcanic eruption. All this seemed merely to have a stimulant effect on the moles, because the next morning the garden was criss-crossed with further runs and mole hills. I bought a dozen more mole smokes and fumigated the whole lawn. More runs appeared the next morning. Our moles were clearly a very tough breed.

The weather did nothing to encourage holidaymaking. Wet days remorselessly followed wet days—long mid-summer days of greyness from the early pink and steely-grey dawn to the slate-grey dusk. There was a velvety softness in those grey days when the lush countryside rested under a blanket of thick protective cloud. We did not even have Wimbledon to watch on television. The matches there were postponed. Meanwhile, like many of our neighbours, Tom was fretting about haymaking. We still had several acres to cut and stack. Luckily, our policy of cutting a few acres at a time was paying off, because it meant we had no hay lying rotting on the ground. Many of our neighbours were less fortunate. Wherever we went we could see fields with row upon row of soaking, yellow, rotting hay. When the rain stopped for a few hours and the sun appeared, we could hear for miles around the tractors pulling the hay tedders that turned and turned the sodden swathes, in a desperate attempt to prevent them rotting.

Arable farmers were no less affected, as high rainfall and low temperatures in June held back the spring-sown crops. At one time a record harvest of sixteen million tons of grain had been forecast, but that was now an abandoned hope.

Fruit farmers were the hardest hit. The radio and the papers told us that our fruit-farming neighbours were suffering badly. In the vast fruit-growing areas of Norfolk and Cambridgeshire there were sixteen consecutive days of rain. Strawberry crops worth four million pounds began to rot in the fields. There was hardly an hour during the early part of July when it was dry enough to pick fruit. This had its reaction on us. Part of the economics of taking paying guests involved my picking pounds and pounds of soft fruit from pick-it-yourself farms. This I stored in the freezer and used to produce luxury puddings which, in fact, only cost a few pence to make. But it did mean that every year I spent several afternoons crawling about on my hands and knees picking strawberries, and then similar periods being scratched and pricked in my pursuit of raspberries.

As I drove down to our nearest pick-your-own farm with the children, the damage caused by the rain was clear. Almost every field was striped with rows of yellow, straw-like ungathered hay, or dotted with sentinels of bales of rotting hay, each a monument to some farmer's dashed hopes of a productive year. Nor was the fruit farm doing much business: the large car park held just two lone cars. Fields that usually echoed with the shrieks of excited children and the pleas of their harassed mothers were silent and still. I parked William in his carrycot under a chestnut tree, hoping the changing pattern of the leaves would keep him quiet while Anthony and I set about collecting as much fruit as possible before the next downpour. For Anthony, strawberry-picking was not so much a matter of picking your own as feeding yourself. He finished the afternoon with exactly five strawberries in his punnet. I do not blame him, for picking the fruit was a most uncomfortable operation. The ground was too wet to kneel on and the fruit itself was a wet mess. Nor was there much fruit, because the lack of sunshine had prevented the crop ripening. And those strawberries that did manage to ripen to red, shiny, jewelled perfection were rapidly weighed down by the rain on the runners and leaves of the plants. On the ground they either rotted or were the target of a vast variety of bugs and grubs. But at least the biggest grub of them all—the human variety that makes a beeline for the spot where anyone is picking industriously and elbows in on them—was absent for once. Anthony and I picked and picked and at the end of the afternoon we had almost fifteen pounds of straw-berries. Enough for puddings for the coming season and for some jam.

These expeditions helped to fill our damp days, but did not do much to relieve our money problems. We were not alone in experiencing a dead holiday season. Seaside hotels and landladies were, it seems, facing the worst summer for more than ten years. The coldest and wettest early summer to affect Europe for over a hundred years had meant either that holidays were not being booked or

were being cancelled or cut short. The papers reported
that in the north of England resorts were facing their
thinnest season for many years, with their takings down
by half. Caterers said they were losing heavily from the
lack of casual trade, those spur-of-the-moment trippers
who, whenever a hot day is forecast, cram into their cars
and head for the coast. In Blackpool landladies reported
people going home after two or three days to avoid
digging too deeply into their pockets to pay for amuse-
ments. So, at least we were not alone in the sufferings of
this new trade we had ventured into.

That solace did not, however, help to pay the bills.
With only scanty bookings in our ledger, we decided the
only solution was to sell a heifer. We picked out Nellie, a
big red and white Hereford lady, as a suitable candidate
for the sale ring. She was one of the beasts we had not
sold the previous autumn. Looking at her we marvelled
at the way animals grow. Standing squarely on four
trunk-like legs she was more like a bison than a heifer. She
seemed to defy the experts. The previous year, when she
had been fed a carefully-balanced menu of protein and
carbohydrate and good hay, she had hardly grown at all.
Last winter she had been shoved in a back shed, nourished
on a handful of barley a day and masses of rough hay, and
yet had doubled in size in six months. We reckoned she
weighed about ten hundredweight and should be worth
at least £320.

When Tom returned from market he was furious.
Nellie had made £50 less than we had expected. I was
astounded. Tom explained that we had been the victims
of one of the oldest tricks of the dealers standing around
the ring. They are always on the lookout for a reason to
criticise an animal so it will be knocked down cheap.
When Nellie had ambled into the ring they started a
whisper that rose to a chant: "She's in calf, she's in calf."
Tom had warranted that Nellie was not in calf, but the

damage was done. She went to one of the dealers for only three quarters of her value.

Tom could not withdraw her from the sale. To do so would seem to confirm that she was in calf. Any attempt to sell her in the market the following week or at another livestock auction would be thwarted by dealers who recognised her and we could not afford to hold her back to the autumn. You are at everyone's mercy when you are short of money.

To cheer myself up I went for a walk outside. On the lawn the moles must have been on double time. In the vegetable garden the leaves of the French beans had a distinctly unhealthy pallor. I examined one closely. It had no roots and nor had most of the others. A mole had tunnelled straight down the row.

I went back into the house and switched on the weather forecast. The weather man was cheerfully confident. A fine high-pressure area was marked on the edge of his chart. The next morning his prediction was confirmed. We woke to lovely sunshine, to find that we had turned one more corner in the hairpin-bend road which is livestock farming.

# Difficult customers

Regulars, those families that returned to the farm every summer like nesting swallows, could be a mixed blessing according to our friends, the Bakers. Harry Baker had warned us in no uncertain terms:

"They can make themselves too much at home, take over the place. They expect special treatment and privileges and monopolise your attention telling you all about what's been happening in their lives since you saw them the previous year. They tend to make the other guests feel like second-class citizens."

But Tom and I welcomed our small, but growing core of regulars with open arms. When the main wave of summer guests at last began to arrive in July, I was hugely relieved—after June's unmitigated disasters—that our first guests were a quiet young couple who had been to Deerpark before and who were particularly fond of the cats. There were no fears about whether they would like the place, no need to reassure them about the road, no introductory warnings about watching the slight step down into the lounge or about the fact that the hot water system would fill two modest baths or one wallowing one.

The week, pleasant and uneventful, healed our painful memories and rekindled our enthusiasm for farm holidaymakers. And we needed all the enthusiasm and cheerfulness we could muster in the next few weeks. Deerpark, like other guest houses, seemed to get a run of guests of the same type and the same foibles. For several weeks almost everyone would be marvellous, and then there were times when they all seemed awful, finicky about their food or needing a great deal of fussing over and attention. That month, most of the guests—not all thank goodness—merited the label 'Handle with Care'. They were not dislikeable people, indeed, all of them proved to be very agreeable, but they needed to be looked after with tact. Our next visitors, the Frazers, who came for the weekend, fitted into this category. They were people of a kind that I expect we will see more often in future years. They were suspicious environmentalists. As keen viewers of television documentaries on the evils of factory farming and on doomwatch predictions of 'agrindustry', they were convinced that all farmers were systematically bleeding the life out of the countryside in the pursuit of bigger and bigger profits. At least Mr. Frazer believed that. Mrs. Frazer, a rather nervous woman who dressed in sweeping Indian cotton skirts and plimsolls, was desperately searching for signs of survival of the old ways in the countryside. She told me triumphantly that at home in Essex she had managed to track down a farm to supply her with free-range eggs and another that reared beef and pork on traditional lines to sell her meat for the freezer. Deerpark won Mrs. Frazer's immediate approval.

"I *do* admire what you are trying to do here," she exclaimed after looking round the farm. Perhaps my bewilderment at the statement showed, because she went on: "I mean the traditional way you are farming."

I was at a loss for a suitable comment. We farmed as we did, because this was all we could afford to do—and because it fitted a place of forty acres. We have never seen ourselves as Luddites of the land, growing food organically, spurning modern machinery and eschewing fertilizers. Our farming methods may be primitive compared with those employed by the big estates, but we are by no means farming freaks. We are merely typical small farmers.

Mr. Frazer was less effusive. He was a big and apparently affable man, but it soon emerged that his bulk concealed a steely cynicism. His faith led him to believe that behind every byre must be an intensive pig unit and behind every barn a battery hen house. He was soon poking around Deerpark looking for signs of intensive farming. But even he had to admit that his search was unrewarding. We were so short of money that Deerpark was under-stocked rather than intensively stocked. Almost in desperation his eyes lit upon the pen of goslings, Anthony's third birthday present. They were in a wired enclosure by the hen house because we wanted to protect them until they were fully grown, from the foxes that raided the farm at night.

"Shouldn't they be in a larger pen?" asked Mr. Frazer sharply as Anthony proudly displayed his pets. "Or are you going to turn them into pâté de foie gras?"

Then he noticed our collie, Lyn, who was dancing around at the end of her chain in a frenzy of frustration at a cat who sat serenely just out of her reach. More evidence of the heartlessness of farmers.

"That dog," he questioned me severely, "Why is she chained up? Is she ever let off?" It was a question people often asked. The film of Thomas Hardy's novel, *Far from the Madding Crowd*, illustrates only too vividly what happens when sheepdogs are left to their own devices. Hardy's shepherd, exhausted with lambing, falls asleep and his dog chases the whole herd of sheep over the edge of the cliff. I explained to Mr. Frazer that sheepdogs chase animals instinctively and when allowed to roam free, will frequently chase and kill sheep, quite apart from getting tangled up with neighbours' dogs and producing un-wanted pups.

I was just trying to escape to the sanctuary of the kitchen when he noticed the pen of baby calves.

"Ah" he gasped with satisfaction, "they're being intensively reared for veal, I suppose."

I had to work hard to keep a straight face. "No, they're being reared on the cows, for beef."

"What do you mean?"

"Not all cows are milked by machine. In this part of the world they are often used to feed calves as an alternative to milk substitute fed from a bucket."

Mr. Frazer looked baffled. When they left the next morning Mrs. Frazer was gleefully clutching a bag of two dozen farm eggs and a jar of crabapple jelly.

Mr. Frazer's face still wore a faint air of disappointment and concern. He seemed torn between his deeply rooted belief that all farming was as heartless as the media portrayed it to be, and the evidence of his own eyes. I could almost hear him wondering whether there were really lots of farms like this? Or was Deerpark simply the odd man out, or perhaps even a put-up job to provide a suitable background for holidaymakers?

Yet I respected the Frazers. For they were on our side, on the side of the small farmer. And the small farmer today is a valuable part of the community. The Common Market had sprung from the desire of the French and the Germans to protect their peasant farms which were even smaller than ours. Indeed many of them are very much smaller. If we were allowed in Britain the same level of rewards for our produce, we would be figuratively, as well as literally, in clover. Certainly it would not be necessary for me to open my home to strangers.

To rid myself of these resentments, I turned to my old hobby of combating the moles. My latest weapon was mothballs. I had taken to these when the mole smokes seemed merely to release clouds of stinking fumes to plague us, but in no way appeared to trouble our underground, uninvited guests. A gardening expert on the radio had assured susceptible listeners like myself that mothballs would work wonders. But not, it seemed, on moles as durable as those in Herefordshire. Nor had another method, proposed by John Hopkins, had any apparent success. He recommended putting crushed gorse into the holes. That just seemed to drive them to greater frenzy a few inches away.

Our next guests were a threesome, a family called the Blakeways. They were a reminder that the victories of Women's Liberation are not yet complete. On the day they arrived, their car drew on to the yard and Mr. Blakeway got out. Even before they had said 'hello', Mr. Blakeway held out his hand imperiously.

"Tobacco," he ordered. "Papers." Mrs. Blakeway rushed round from the passenger seat and pressed both items into his hand. Mr. Blakeway then proceeded to roll a cigarette.

"I'll show you your rooms," I said after greetings had been exchanged. Mr. Blakeway and Tommy, their twelve-year-old son, followed me. I paused at the foot of the stairs. I showed them the lounge and the bathroom. Where was Mrs. Blakeway? Mr. Blakeway was fidgeting with impatience.

"I'd better see what's happened to Mrs. Blakeway," I said. "I think we must have lost her."

Mrs. Blakeway was still darting around the car, unloading bits and pieces, popping in and out of it like a pigeon outside a dovecote. I grabbed a couple of cases and led the way into the house. At the foot of the stairs the female baggage bearers halted.

"Take this," Mrs. Blakeway ordered Tommy and motioned to one of the suitcases. There was a strangled sound from Tommy.

"Oo aah, aah no," he exclaimed, but after a sharp altercation with his mother he seized the case with bad grace and trundled upstairs, with it knocking as much paintwork off the banisters as possible. I viewed from the top of the stairs Mr. Blakeway following the reluctant Tommy, empty-handed except for his cigarette, and Mrs. Blakeway, almost hidden in a mound of suitcases, bringing up the rear.

"Would you like a cup of tea?" I asked to stop myself laughing. Mr. Blakeway was in no doubt. "Yes, I would," he replied with an equal emphasis on each word. "We didn't stop. *She* usually puts a flask in. But *she* didn't this time. I can't think why. *Women!*"

When I took the tea into the lounge Mrs. Blakeway had materialised again.

"Oh, no," she wailed, "I've left all our washing things at home. I've left our sponge bags on the pouffe."

Mr. Blakeway exploded this time. "*Women!*"

Half an hour later I served the supper. Mr. Blakeway and Tommy were sitting at the table with the intent expressions of greyhounds in starting traps. Where *was* Mrs. Blakeway? I looked out of the window. She was still unpacking the car all on her own. I sighed slightly under my breath. I could foresee difficulties.

It proved in fact impossible to get the whole family to sit down to a meal together. At nine o'clock each morning the males would seat themselves at the table promptly for breakfast. But there would be no Mrs. Blakeway. On the first day I hung on for ten minutes waiting for her. Father and son began to get restless so I asked them for their order.

"At last," exclaimed Mr. Blakeway, "I'm starving." I served the two of them first. Ten minutes later Mrs. Blakeway came into the kitchen to collect her breakfast. This pattern followed day after day.

With this rich variety of human nature sitting at our

table, I was beginning to nod my head sagely when people asked what it was like taking holiday guests, and then remark as enigmatically as I could: "You certainly see life."

Yet they were still essential to our survival. Certainly they were better than another venture we tried that summer.

Since poultry prices were then good, Tom turned his attention to hatching chicks. In the economy of the countryside the poultry house is normally the woman's exclusive domain. Until recently many farmers' wives received very little housekeeping money but generated their own income by making butter, selling eggs and rearing table birds from raw materials on the farm. But fowl, I had to admit after four years of farming, were not my forte. They were not Tom's either, but he had taken them over now that I was busy with the baby and the guests.

We needed more hens, and so Tom decided to breed them. But we were to discover that there is more to hatching eggs than putting a broody hen on top of them. Hens are bred nowadays to lay an egg a day for one year in carefully regulated conditions on a controlled diet. They are not bred to hatch and rear chicks. Only our bantam hens, who had not had their natural instincts bred out of them, would disappear for several weeks and then emerge on the yard with half a dozen fluffy chicks. But what we needed were more large hens to lay large eggs. Our first attempt at chick hatching was a total washout; most of the eggs failed to hatch and the two chicks that did appear were quickly sat upon and suffocated by their incompetent mother. The next sitting was barely more successful. The hen was sitting safely in a box in the hen house, but to our bewilderment the eggs kept disappearing from under her. Where were they going? There was no sign of the eggs, no hint of smashed eggshell or chicks. One morning when I was cooking the breakfast and cracked an egg into the pan, an embryonic chick splashed into the fat. Realisation dawned. The hen was pushing the eggs from under her and shoving them out from under the box, in amongst the other newly-laid eggs.

Finally one broody hen did manage to hatch two chicks. But they too were doomed. Anthony came into the vegetable garden clutching one and chanting: "Baby chick, baby chick." Three year olds have great strength but tend to be clumsy. My enthusiastic son had throttled the chick. The other was no luckier; it escaped into the henhouse and was immediately set upon by the other hens. Man's inhumanity to man pales into insignificance compared to the fowl world's murderous inclinations. They have a rigid social order, the pecking order, and any bird, such as a chick separated from its mother, which is unable to hold its own, is immediately set upon by the other hens.

We tried again. This time Tom isolated the nesting box in one of the loose boxes. Three weeks later his efforts were rewarded with seven successful hatchings. Four met with accidents, such as falling into buckets of water or being stepped on by calves. But the other three survived—two cockerels and a beautiful vain white hen. Tom fed them on a diet of breadcrumbs mixed with hard boiled egg and they flourished. We enjoyed watching the little procession of proud mother leading her trio of fluffy chicks round the yard, teaching them how to peck and scratch for food. But before long the fowls' murderous instincts began to show in a vicious form of sibling rivalry. Both cockerels would attack the little hen, plucking out all her neck feathers and most of the body ones. She began to look ready plucked for the oven. As soon as the beautiful white feathers had grown again the two cockerels would have another go at her. No, poultry did not seem the answer.

In the house we had other problems. We were accommodating a couple who moved around in a strange smelling aroma. It had an Oriental tang to it and we wondered if they were smoking pot. The whole house began to smell of it, particularly in the upstairs passage. It was an odour we could not identify—a thick cloying smell like hot house flowers. Yet there was no tobacco smell associated with it. We sought enlightenment from a neighbour, Jean, who had a specialised knowledge of plants such as 'Hereford Green'.

"Take a sniff," I invited. "What do you reckon?"

"No, it's not pot. That has quite a distinctive smell. You can't miss it. But all the same, it's a smell you associate with hash. I know! It's petuli oil!"

I was mystified. "That's a new one on me."

"When the Haight–Ashbury thing was on, Flower Power and all that, people used to put petuli oil on themselves to mask the smell of pot. You didn't have to wash either because it covers up B.O. too. Some people still use it. They think it has a nice smell. A lot of health shops stock it."

We both burst out laughing at the thought. "Isn't it awful!"

When the Smellies, as we privately called them, had left I tried to banish the persistent smell from the room. I washed the sheets but it was still there. Then I washed the blankets; still the reek of petuli hung in the air. I laundered the curtains and the bedcover; it still lingered, particularly when the room had been shut up for several days. It must have soaked into the wallpaper. Even now when I go into the room I swear I can detect a whiff of the heavy Oriental smell of petuli.

This laundry work was the more difficult because the weather had changed again. Sun had given way to rain so heavy that I could not open the windows. The last few days of July and the first week of August were the wettest for forty years. Statistics cannot convey just how hard that rain fell. For four long days it came down heavily and continuously. It rained from the east in thick constant clouds. Sky, fields, trees were swallowed in a dense clinging mist that wrapped the world in clouds of damp and cold. Water ran everywhere: it dripped off the gutters that were overwhelmed with rain, it poured off trees, it gushed over the fields filling up ditches that had been dry since the great storm two months before.

On this occasion, though, the weather did not deter holidaymakers. August, with its school holidays, is the peak month. It is the only time many people can take a break and they stick to their arrangements come hell or, as in this case, high water. In preparation for the rush I drove over to Hereford to stock up from the cash-and-carry on the industrial estate. Like so many of these developments throughout Britain, this estate is a ghost town. But unlike the traditional ghost towns of the gold rush days, Hereford's industrial estate is haunted not by spectres of times past, but by the shapes of things that might have been. Set in the valley below the green wooded hills of south Herefordshire, it looks as derelict as a deserted army camp. Plots for factories that have never been built are bisected by roads pitted with potholes or split with sprouting grass. I stopped the car on one corner of the half-used, half-deserted road. On some plots there might be an old Nissen hut, on others a factory or warehouse. Several have been returned temporarily to agriculture and cows graze beside the new factories. But most of the plots are reverting, perhaps permanently, to nature. And how quickly nature reasserts itself across any fields which farmers stop tending. Dusty docks and thistles move in, ragwort and willow herb spring up. Rambling roses shamble over the wasteland, brambles entwine their prickly tendrils over clumps of bracken and thistles. In this wilderness, the most poignant sight is that of the fire hydrants. They stand erect and modern, a reminder that here the main services are all laid down, ready to help Britain move into a new industrial era, ready to make a reality of the attempt to graft light industry on to impoverished old market towns. But then came the oil crisis, the three-day week and the world recession. Swiftly these put a halt to peripheral industrial developments such as this one near Hereford, leaving them as up-to-the-minute monuments of our industrial lameness. It reminded me with a jolt of the root cause of the problems on our own farm. We too were battling against the same forces which had stunted and blunted these hopes of a decade ago. But we at least had held our ground, had hit upon one means of paying our way, however hard that way might be.

My halt was brief. I had a full household to shop for and a full order book for the next few weeks. I switched on the car engine and continued my journey to the cash-and-carry.

# There's no accounting for tastes

A solitary swallow was perched on the powerline slung across the yard between the old barn and the farmhouse. Ignoring the heavy skies and chilling north wind that had sent its companions south three months earlier than normal, it sat blinking and apparently content. I stopped and watched the bird for a few seconds on my way to the barn with a bucket of scraps and biscuits for the dogs. Perhaps the swallow was a good omen, perhaps the weather was about to perk up again. It was time something happened, for the renewed bad weather had coincided with a family of guests whom it seemed impossible to please. I looked sadly into the dog bucket. At least our three canine workers, Zara the Alsatian, Risky the terrier and Lyn the border collie were in for a treat that evening. Nestling amongst a mountain of fried eggs, of almost whole rashers of bacon, of slices of bread and scatterings of fresh peas and beans, were four lamb chops, two of them untouched and two barely half-eaten. They were English lamb chops, from a hogget—a year-old lamb. It was the sweetest and tastiest of all meat, of a kind now almost impossible to buy from a butcher. Our current guests, the Maynards, had rejected them that evening. The scene was still clear in my mind. I had gone into the sitting room to clear away the main course. They had drawn the curtains tightly against the watery sun that broke through the clouds from time to time and on the window-sill a transistor radio was belting out the Top Ten.

Mr. and Mrs. Maynard looked up cheerfully as they heard the door open. Their daughter, Dawn, stared into the middle distance with the expression of fixed misery that I had become accustomed to seeing on the faces of teenage daughters spending a holiday with their parents. Granny Maynard was still fiddling around with her food.

In front of them the lamb chops lay on the plates almost unmolested. When I served them up I had thought how delicious the chops looked, grilled so that the fat was brown and crisp, yet leaving the meat juicy with a faintly discernible blush of pink. I may have been a rotten pastry maker, but I knew I could cook meat.

Mr. Maynard was not one of those who did not like to make a fuss. He came to the point at once.

"We can't eat these, dear. They're raw. Much too rare for us." A thought struck him. "Do you always cook lamb chops like this? We'd have liked them done another full fifteen minutes." Then he added sadly. "Such a pity to waste good meat by not cooking it properly."

I apologised. Once again I muttered to myself that the customer is always right, even if he does want his lamb chops processed into hardboard. If there is one adage you soon appreciate in the holiday trade, it is 'there's no accounting for tastes'. In the kitchen I cut into one of the offending chops in case I had not thawed them out sufficiently after taking them from the freezer, but there was no sign of rawness. I was learning one important lesson in my new career as a caterer; at least a third of our guests liked their food 'properly' cooked, which meant over-cooked.

I took the raspberry meringues into the lounge. There would be no complaint about that. If there is one passion that unites the British of all classes and from all regions, it is their love of puddings. Any combination of fruit and goo—pastry, sponge, cake, meringues, cheesecake, mousse—topped off with whipped cream, is sure to be hugely popular. Mr. Maynard's angular face lit up with delight. Granny was still preoccupied with her main course.

"Don't worry about Granny," Mr. Maynard motioned with his head towards the old woman. He and his wife always talked as though she were in another room. "Granny's a slow eater. It's her teeth. They don't fit properly. And she's got gumboils." He raised his voice: "Innit right, Gran, you've got trouble with your teeth?"

Granny grasped my arm and shouted in my ear as I bent down to take her plate. "Always had trouble with this set. That's why I can't eat my crusts. You don't mind, do you, dear? It's not that I don't like the bread, it's my gumboils."

Nothing seemed to please the Maynards. They had arrived at 11 o'clock in the morning and had been annoyed that the rooms were not ready. They eschewed all vegetables, disliked meat with even the smallest border of fat (including bacon) and avoided all bread crusts, sending the slices back to the kitchen with a window pecked in the middle. They complained loudly because tea was not included free of charge with the evening meal. Such people, I had heard, were known in the holiday trade as 'grockles'. They demanded a great deal of extra attention and service, but were never really satisfied.

If the house dogs were doing very well on the guests' left-overs, the other animals were doing too well. When we first began our guest house enterprise I wrote out a card in red capital letters: ON NO ACCOUNT SHOULD GUESTS FEED THE ANIMALS. I put this, together with the typewritten list of information, on the back of the bedroom doors. But by this second summer the notices had become tatty and dogeared, so I took them down. In any case, the notices seemed rather unfriendly and, I thought, unnecessary. No one surely would dream of feeding farm animals. I could not have been more mistaken. As soon as the notices disappeared into the dustbin the guests were feeding all the animals on the farm. The Blakeways put the scraps from their plates into a napkin and fed them to Lyn, our working collie, after supper. Children purchased and fed pony nuts to Alice, our Shetland pony, without a word to anyone. Everyone gave titbits to the horses in the field and Mrs. Blakeway gave Zara, the Alsatian, a biscuit every time she got out of the car.

Tom got increasingly wrathful. The animals housed in the barn, like the calves, were fed on scientifically formulated diets that were not designed to be supplemented with biscuits and sweets. Working sheepdogs can grow silly and unworkable when petted and fed titbits. Snacks between meals have been the ruin of many a horse. Not only does it make them quite literally bite the hand that feeds them (or they think is going to feed them) but it can lead to injuries. People unused to horses usually stand with the fence between them and the horse when offering a titbit. The horse stretches his head forward and cuts the skin under his neck on the top strand of wire in his eagerness. Luckily none of our animals had yet suffered any such ill effects. Nevertheless, I quickly re-typed the notices and stuck them back on the bedroom doors. But it is a strange passion, this desire to feed other people's animals. Perhaps it is that people feel they can only make contact with an animal by offering it something to eat.

Most of our guests to date had, however, one characteristic in common. They loved to talk to us, to any fellow guests, to the regulars in the Fox and Pheasant. But the Berrens were different. They set about quickly establishing an invisible frontier between us, the servers, and them the served. When I offered my usual "Did you sleep well?" I met that frozen stare that emanates from people who are interrupted in the course of an important conversation. A typical meal time exchange would be:

"I think we'll paint the living room Aphrodite—Oh, we'll have grapefruit juice—And we could have a mushroom carpet."

From him. "Bertie never seems to be able to achieve a meaningful relationship." A quick glance up. "Biscuits and cheese for two."—"He seems to have reached a rapport with Ruth though."

I found it increasingly difficult to mouth the necessary morning pleasantries, the bright "Good morning. The forecast is jolly good for this afternoon." Usually the response was a distracted glance and 'Urr um um.' Yet they seemed to be happy with the place and happy with their holiday and that was all that mattered.

But their manner did upset Anthony. On their first evening he rushed into the lounge and did his party piece. "Good evening, guests!"

Instead of the normal reply, a roar of "Good evening, Anthony," there was a stoney silence. He tried again. Both the Berrens, who were in their early thirties, stared fixedly at their plates as if someone had made an antisocial noise. Anthony looked at me in desperation. Making soothing noises I took his hand and led him to the door. As I paused to open it Anthony had one last try. This time Mrs. Berrens half-turned and looked up at us . . . and giggled. As the week wore on, I realised their attitude was not arrogance, but shyness. But Anthony was barely three and was stunned by the total rejection by these two strangers who had moved into his home. He started to shout in his sleep again and at about two o'clock the next morning he woke up and got into my bed with me.

None of us would have slept easy in our beds if we had

known what we were in for with the family we were expecting the next week. They arrived about half an hour after I had had one more attack on the moles. They were called the Kentlands and there were three of them— parents in their late thirties and a fourteen-year-old son called Jerry. They were cheerful and friendly, but after supper that evening I began to suspect that Jerry was going to test our nerves. He had curiously restless, darting eyes that made me uneasy. When I asked Mrs. Kentland if there were any dishes she and her family did not like, I realised Jerry was not the straightforward teenager he looked. Before answering my query Mrs. Kentland looked nervously at her husband.

"Err, Jerry. He's an egg and chips boy. He's at that stage—you know what they're like. I mean he wouldn't eat any of those potatoes . . ." she motioned to the plate half-full of sauté potatoes, "because they're not chips. And he doesn't eat vegetables. At home I cook two meals—one for us and one for Jerry."

I gave Jerry a hard look. At that time I was preparing three separate meals each evening, first, one for William, then one for the guests and finally a snack for Tom, Anthony and myself. I had no intention of cooking a fourth meal for a spoilt teenager who was determined to make people run round in circles for him.

"And tomatoes," Mrs. Kentland was continuing the list of Jerry's dislikes, "definitely no tomatoes for Jerry." She finished in a horrified tone.

Jerry's table manners, I soon learnt, also left much to be desired. After the first course he would jump out of his chair, dive out of the door and disappear into the lavatory. One morning I noticed his egg and bacon were untouched when I started to clear away the dishes.

"Is Jerry all right?" I asked, wondering if he, like some of our other guests, had fallen victim to the effects of Herefordshire cider.

His father, who was clearly finding the holiday a strain, replied tersely: "He went to the toilet after his cornflakes and when he came back to the table complained that the egg and bacon were cold."

Every evening Jerry made a fuss by refusing the pudding in a manner both disgusted and disdainful. "What's on the menu for pudding today?" he would ask. When told, his response would be: "Ugh. I hate chocolate mousse. Never did like strawberry flan. Rhubarb crumble—horrible." One day he unbent a little. "I wouldn't mind some jam roly-poly," he said, in response to the question of whether he would like apple pie.

"Sorry. We don't do special diets here," I replied gaily.

His mother added: "If we were at home I'd go off and make him one. I'm that much of a fool."

I went back to the kitchen to give William his favourite caramel cream and pondered on the extraordinary way people use food as a weapon in their battle for affection.

Mrs. Kentland was so worried that her son was not eating enough that I relented and served up chips on alternate days. On the second occasion I was surprised to see half a dish of chips left.

"Sorry," apologised Mrs. Kentland, "Jerry only had one chip. He had egg and chips for his lunch." Clearly I was out of favour with Jerry.

His lack of appetite, I suspected, owed much to his lack of exertion. Every morning after breakfast the television was switched on and Jerry would watch steadily for a couple of hours. Cartoons were his particular favourite. Sitting beside him was my son, Anthony, who thought this departure from the normal routine was wonderful. It took me months afterwards to stop his morning viewing. Jerry also seemed to need mollycoddling in his bedroom. Despite the warm weather I was surprised to see the electric fire plugged into the socket every time I bent down to connect the vacuum cleaner.

To our relief the family was out of the house for most of the evening, spending their time in the Fox and Pheasant. On all but two occasions they took Jerry with them.

The day after they left Tom happened to be in the Fox and Pheasant and was chatting to the landlady, Mrs. Carson.

"Odd boy that, you had staying last week. His mother said they had to bring him down here every night for fear of the damage he might do if he was left on his own at Deerpark. At home he's burnt the furnishings with acid from his chemistry set and ruined the curtains by jerking ink at them from his fountain pen. They thought he might set the place on fire. It seems he likes playing with fire. Apparently he's been bullied a lot at school, because he's clever and he gets out of hand."

A week later Tom and I were moving the chest of drawers in the room Jerry had occupied. Behind it were five charred spills of paper. Jerry had not been using the electric fire merely to heat his room. He had needed it in his experiments to test how much oxygen lurked behind the chest of drawers. Luckily for us, there was not much there. The wallpaper and the skirting board were slightly scorched, but no real harm had resulted. Outside Tom discovered that into the thick tyres of the blue tractor had been scratched the initials 'J.K.'

The weather was still abominable. It was so wet that William Hill offered odds of five to one to anyone who could forecast the first dry spell of forty-eight hours in London. On August 12th hundreds of punters had their hopes dashed when it rained after an interval of forty-seven hours—the longest dry spell we had enjoyed for over a fortnight. Then, just to try our patience a bit further, the next group of visitors cancelled their holiday two days before they were due to arrive. We had no time to re-advertise the rooms. Although I was entitled to two thirds of the money they would have paid, they flatly refused to pay anything, saying the ten per cent deposit they had sent was adequate recompense.

But suddenly, the weather improved at last. August bloomed into a rich lush month with lavish, almost tropical vegetation spreading over the countryside. Normally it is a month which seems tarnished and blowsy. The atmosphere is often humid, and skies are overcast with low gloomy clouds mooning over dusty fields full of coarse vegetation running to seed and turning brown. But now it was as though an extra month had been added to the calendar. I thought of it as the true season of full summer. Vivid colours were slapped on to the landscape. Grass grew with renewed vigour, corn ripened with green heads atop of yellow straw, fields of sugar beet were a mass of thick juicy leaves like plants from an equatorial rain forest, full rivers with banks carpeted with wild flowers swept through the well-grassed water meadows.

The combine harvesters which had been waiting in barley fields ready to snatch what they could between showers, began to work confidently and steadily.

Nor was the house completely empty for the week. Since this was the peak holiday season we began to get people seeking a bed for odd nights. They were referred from the Fox and Pheasant or from other bed and break-fast farms in the area that were full up. It was to bring a change to the rhythm of life. We entered a time when we never knew whether we would have the house to ourselves for the night or whether I would be cooking a three-course meal with fifteen minutes' notice. I loved it. People 'off the road' were generally friendly and appreciative, thankful for a bed and a meal and delighted at discovering such a beautiful staging post in the wilderness.

The first of these 'casuals' were a man and his wife who rang up and booked a meal, bed and breakfast and said they would arrive in half an hour. I whisked around the house with a duster and vacuum cleaner and was just congratulating myself on how well I was managing, when Anthony came round the corner by the diesel tank. At first I thought his appearance was a trick of light because the sun was shining in my eyes. His arms seemed to be shiny. More than that, they were black and shiny. Then with mounting horror I realised what had happened. His arms and his shirt and trousers *were* black and shiny; he had sunk his arms into a bucket of bitumastic paint that the men painting the barn roofs had left behind. I let out a screech. Cleaning him up would take hours and I would get covered with the stuff in the process. This was a job for Father, I decided, and set off with Anthony to the field where Tom was mowing thistles.

Tom told me not to make a fuss, that he would soon clean up our tar baby. But it was not so simple. We tried industrial cleanser first, which we used for removing dabs of paint from our hands, but it made little impression on a thick coating of bitumastic. White spirit was no good either. In desperation we led Anthony into the toolshed and smeared him in tractor grease with a grease gun. We then wiped the grease off with a piece of old sheet, and repeated the process. After about ten minutes some pinkish skin appeared. At last he was clean enough to be put into the bath. By the time the guests arrived, the situation was more or less under control and I was able to get the worst of the grease off the bathroom while they were making short work of gammon steak, chips and peas.

We found these over-nighters such a pleasant bonus that we decided to fit in as many as we could. To do this, however, we realised that we must have a second dining table.

So deep rooted, it seems, is the territorial instinct, that people away from their homes—however friendly they may be to new acquaintances—feel uneasy facing them at the same table at meal times. They will readily sit around in the same sitting room, take a stroll up and down in the garden together. But at meal times they like to have their own separate family tables, even though they will talk across to each other from table to table. And there are those too, who when holidaying alone, like to read a book or newspaper at meals rather than make bright conversation with other diners.

We borrowed from my parents a post-war utility model table which was just right for the job. But its arrival baffled my son. Accustomed like all farm children to the big farm kitchen table being the natural centre of life, he demanded, "Why don't they all sit at one table?"

He was unimpressed by my explanations.

In the end I was reduced to answering. "They don't like sitting with people they don't know. Why? They *just* don't."

The fine weather transformed the task of providing farm holidays. The sun seemed to light up Deerpark in the way the lights turn a stage set into a warm, rich, alive scene. The greenness and fertility of the surrounding fields and woods, the richness of the purple slopes of the Black Mountains and of the Brecon Beacons to the west, the dark green mass of Radnor Forest, provided our visitors with the country peace and beauty they had hoped for. At night, tiny bats dived and swooped around the eaves of the house, at times we even heard a nightingale, its voice the perfect counterpart to the warm fragrance of night-scented stock from our small but well-filled front garden. The only snag of the finer, drier weather was the reappearance of the moles, who started to tunnel deeper into the lawn and to chuck up even larger hills of earth. Though the garden was by now well and truly planted with mothballs, there was no sign of our underground labourers quitting in disgust at the smell. But we kept up the treatment, if only because we could think of nothing else to do. One morning I looked out of the bedroom window to see Anthony, clad only in his pyjama jacket, clutching the bag of mothballs. Alarmed that he had mistaken them for sweets, I asked him what he was doing. Surprised at such an unnecessary question, he answered: "I'm killing the ruddy moles for you."

My baby son was, however, proving less co-operative. He had developed a firm habit of waking up twice a night, cheerfully but wakefully noisy. In doing so, he robbed me of what I most wanted—sleep. I learnt to sleep deeply, in snatches, but I also began to have nightmares about cooking and serving hordes and hordes of holidaymakers. One dream stuck in my mind. I was serving a table full of people in the living room and when I went thankfully back to the kitchen there were yet more people sitting round the kitchen table all demanding attention. "I want some more toast." "Any more butter?" "Is there any more tea?" "I want an iron." (An iron? What did they want an iron for? Puzzling.)

A few days later that dream was translated into reality. It was August Bank Holiday. We had things nicely in hand, with a pleasant family of four booked in for a week. After lunch the phone rang and a breathless voice asked if I could possibly squeeze in two adults and four children. The idea of 'squeezing' in six people stunned me for a moment. We had one double room vacant, but that was all. Then I thought of our caravan, stationed in the yard to serve as the farm office, now that the guests had taken over the living room. I offered the four berths in the caravan and they were thankfully accepted.

Tom was walking the stallion up and down the farmyard in the sunshine.

"We've six more coming in tonight," I told him. He stared at me with the same startled look of disbelief that comes into my eyes when he tells me he has bought six calves for £100 apiece in the market. Then he saw I was serious. "Phew. I'll try and give you a hand. We ought to be able to cope."

The caravan had its own washbasin, so I topped up its water supply and dealt with the further problem of hygiene by putting one of the chamber pots into it. How ten people would all manage to share one bathroom did not bear thinking about. They would have to organise it amongst themselves.

We were at supper that evening when a vehicle roared by the window and swept into the yard. We caught a brief glimpse of a station wagon festooned with children's heads and arms hanging out of the windows. Our new arrivals were clearly not the sort of people who crept up the road with their hearts in their mouths for fear of damaging the car's exhaust.

Children exploded out of the car and careered round the farmyard like a bunch of cattle escaping from a pen. They were delighted with the prospect of a night in a caravan. Their vitality and gusto seemed to sweep aside all problems—mine as well as theirs.

I gave the Reeses, as these last-minute arrivals were called, the choice of an eight-thirty or a nine-thirty breakfast. Since the regular guests ate at nine o'clock, I could then cook breakfast in two shifts. The Reeses plumped for a nine-thirty meal. But at eight-twenty the next morning Mr. Reese and the four children emerged from the bathroom.

"Do you think we could have an eight-thirty breakfast after all? I don't think my monkeys can wait another hour."

What from another family might have seemed an intolerable burden from the bright-eyed Reeses seemed just a bit more zest added to life. Of course I could. I juggled bacon, eggs, tea, toast, tomatoes, cornflakes and orange juice for the next hour. Tom nobly played his part holding William and carrying trays hither and thither. Young voices piped up: "Any more toast?" "I want some more tea." "Where's the marmalade?" Above the bedlam I could hear the educated syllables of Mr. Reese: "I want an iron to press my cricket flannels." An iron. And this, I swear, was a week *later* than my dream.

At ten o'clock the over-nighters had left and the regulars had departed for the day. Tom and I sat down to a cup of coffee at the scrubbed kitchen table. We looked at the Reeses' cheque. Maybe it was a mad rush, but that was the vet's bill paid anyway.

That Bank Holiday was the forerunner of many more nights when we packed the house full of people and rushed about from seven o'clock in the morning until long after midnight. I was surprised to find it more exhilarating than exhausting, a stimulating change in the remorseless rhythm of our normal farming existence.

Farming is a life of routine. The need to look after animals that are utterly dependent on you imposes a daily round of essential unchanging work. Bank Holidays, Sundays, Christmas, Easter, are just like any other day of the week, except that the shops are closed if you run out of cow cake or six-inch nails. Now, although we ourselves were not on holiday (indeed quite the opposite) these holiday weekends became times we looked forward to, times to plan for in the long months of winter, times when we knew we would have to have all our wits and our energies about us.

That August Bank Holiday also marked a return of ordinary, nice people as our guests. The 'grockles' must have been going elsewhere. One friendly, cheerful family with two young children could hardly contain their joy when Tom allowed them to help feed the stock. They restored Anthony to his former, perky self, by letting him join in searches with a metal detector they had with them. They unearthed heaps of scrap which Anthony hoarded carefully, but found no treasure. The mother of another family insisted on giving me a hand, clearing the table after meals, bringing the trays out to the kitchen and hanging out the washing. She wanted to do more, but I knew I had to steel myself against accepting such offers. A bargain was a bargain, and our part of it was to provide a holiday.

We were still taking in people who turned up out of nowhere. At times we felt like participants in a play: who would sit down for dinner at this remote farmhouse tonight? The quite unexpected bonus was that everyone, whoever they were, seemed to get on famously. People did not seem to mind the slightly cramped conditions. Indeed the question of sharing a bathroom seemed to help weld a houseful of guests into a happy group. Perhaps nothing brings people together more quickly than facing a common problem. Anyway, they often commented: "It's such a friendly atmosphere." Tom and I would nod our ready agreement, though we realised, rather guiltily, that we had been so busy that we had done no more than pass the time of day with them. Nor did the extra people, to my surprise, create a corresponding amount of extra strain. For one thing we found ourselves relieved of the worry about whether they were satisfied. Having plenty of company seemed to make them less censorious. Moreover, they talked to each other rather than pouncing on Tom or me as a captive audience. No longer did I have to back tactfully out of the room muttering: "Excuse me. Must save the chops."

Best of all, the complaints about the road stopped. Instead it became a lively topic of discussion. Occasionally, when serving the meal I heard snatches of conversation:

"I found that half-brick that sticks up in the middle of the road by the gate. I knocked a bit off it."

"I know the one you mean. I find by driving to the right slightly I can avoid it."

A pause.

"I hit a tree root today."

The fine weather stayed with us well into September. It was a complete contrast to conditions two years before, when rainstorms had lashed the country during the August Bank Holiday, to make, to our relief, the end of the great drought and the end of the summer. We had the strong feeling now that the summer was only half over. There was certainly no hint yet of autumn. Skies were a clear singing blue; grass was strong and thick like spring grass. In the mornings the big oaks on the front pasture stood out strong and green, still in full sap. Indeed the trees looked fresher than they had in July, because a second set of leaves opened out at the end of the twigs. The fields of the Marches sparkled and glinted, and, further westward, the Black Mountains were hued in soft blue. From the front pastures the outlines of the hills stretching towards south Herefordshire looked romantically misty, like an unexpectedly-sighted coastline.

Unfortunately, the moles seemed to like the weather too and were still working away in the lawn with immense dedication. An elderly guest offered some advice.

"I had one in my lawn. Tried every damned thing without success. Then one day I saw the grass moving so I jumped on it. Killed the brute stone dead. Only way to get rid of the blighters." I took to watching the lawn out of the corner of my eye while I cleaned the house. Occasionally I would catch sight of a rippling movement beneath the turf and I would rush out of the house and stamp on it. But the moles remained elusive. Perhaps I didn't carry the necessary weight.

September on a farm is not however just a season of mists and mellow fruitfulness. It is also the month of the straw harvest and straw in bales means heavy work.

Since the weather looked settled there was no need to rush to lug our straw in. Tom and I decided we could manage to cart it ourselves if we worked at a steady pace, bringing in one or two loads of 150 bales every day. Even so, it took some contriving to fit in the job of carting straw with that of looking after two children and two elderly guests.

The straw had been left in neat rows in the field by the combine harvester. Getting down to collect it was like organising a travelling circus. I drove one tractor which hauled a trailer on which was perched Anthony. William was strapped firmly to my chest in the baby sling. Tom came behind driving the second tractor, which was fitted with a hydraulic lift. The lift had as its cargo the carrycot. Once we were in the field, William was off-loaded into the carrycot and parked, usually protesting noisily, under a handy tree. Tom and I then loaded the trailer with bales, while Anthony made use of the other piles of bales as a jungle gym.

On the first day I took one load back on my own, while Tom remained to continue baling the straw. Two pairs of eyes watched me from the living-room window as I sweated and struggled to unload the bales and pile them in the big Dutch barn. When the 150th bale was in the barn I reverted to my role as landlady, went into the house and asked the guests if they would like a cup of tea.

"Is that the lot?" asked the elderly gentleman with a sympathetic smile, "I expect you are glad to have done with it."

I thought of the remaining 1,000 bales standing in tumps of six in the field half a mile away.

"Few more to come yet," I told him.

That week we loaded, unloaded and stacked bales from ten in the morning until ten at night. By Friday we had had enough. We left the last load on the trailer and threw a tarpaulin over it in case it rained.

"We'll unload it on Sunday," said Tom. It was still there at Christmas. It was in top-top condition and we fed it to the stock as a Christmas dinner.

On Saturday morning when the elderly couple left they presented us with a pound box of chocolates. Tom and I ate the lot, with Anthony's help, with our morning coffee.

But if farming and running a guest house could, with luck, be interlocked, the pattern became more complicated when child-rearing had to be fitted in as well. William had started teething and was keeping me up most of the night.

"Teeth," said one neighbour, "painful to get, painful to keep and painful to lose."

"It's not surprising children kick up a fuss when they're teething. Look at what toothache can do to grown men," added John Hopkins. "You know Pop Sadler? He's got the flashiest set of false teeth in the village now. But he used to pull his own teeth out. Didn't like dentists. That was his back teeth. He knocked his front teeth out by accident. They stuck out, protruded like. He was cycling back from Hamfield one night with half a hundredweight of spuds under his arm when his coat caught in the wheel spokes and he fell off and knocked his teeth out."

I did not think that was the cure for William's trouble. I tried every product on the market to tackle the pain but nothing seemed effective.

Fatigue now began to hit me hard. Perhaps it was because the end of the tourist season was in sight and I could begin to admit to myself how weary I was. From the early summer onwards I had progressed through all stages of tiredness. I had come out in spots, been irritable and bad tempered and suffered from aching knees and sore feet. Now I was wide-eyed and light-headed with fatigue. Sometimes as I was driving back from town with a car full of groceries I would feel the delicious peace of sleep creeping over me. The green wooded hills bordering the Marches would grow soft and fuzzy . . . I would wind down the window and breathe deeply as the cool air swept into the car. Only a few more weeks to go.

The fine weather went on and on. And the visitors kept coming, keen to enjoy the last few days of summer before the long winter arrived. Even by the third week of September there were few signs of autumn—not a golden leaf to be seen. Our vegetable garden was bursting with produce and in every spare moment I harvested cauliflowers, beans, broccoli and carrots and put them in the freezer. In East Anglia farmers were talking of a glut of Brussels sprouts that would have to be destroyed because housewives did not want them even at knockdown prices. Despite my lack of sleep, the warm balmy days with the strong sun shining out of a clear blue sky kept my spirits high.

By eight o'clock each morning the countryside had emerged from the overnight mist as if from a dream and the clear air and bright sunshine banished all thoughts of the cold months ahead. Yet the cool of the dew-laden early mornings was a reminder that we were living on borrowed time, that, beyond a short autumn, winter was mercilessly creeping up on us.

Hedgerows hinted at this hardship to come. They were purple and red with fruit; elder bushes leant over under the weight of their tart berries; brambles were weighed down with blackberries; crab apples scattered their fruit on the ground with wasteful abandon; wild damsons were there for the taking, and sloes, hips and red hawthorn berries. Though people talked of a hard winter after such an autumn of plenty, we were sceptical. We had known other fruitful autumns and yet had not seen a cold winter for fifteen years.

Above all, the evenings of that Indian summer of 1978 stay in mind as one of those rare golden periods in life.

The air was calm and warm with only the dry rustle of kittens in the straw disturbing the stillness. Tom and I often walked through the thick grass of the front pasture to the dewpond, the focus of the farm. There we watched the cattle grazing contentedly on grass that in any other year would have long lost its goodness. Looking back towards the house we could see Clee Hill in the background, high and clear, part of ancient Britain. Golden sunsets lit up the sky and there was a moment every evening when the dying rays of the sun steeped the horse chestnut trees in a deep, glowing bronze.

# Into the black – just

When the alarm clock hurtled me into consciousness at six-thirty in the morning on the first Thursday in October, I realised with a jolt how dark it still was. Winter was approaching fast, even if the fine weather was still with us. With that in mind, Tom and I had decided to sell our first bunch of twelve heifers before the grass lost its goodness and before we had to start supplementing their diet with expensively purchased barley. Though the income from the guests—and we still had one couple with us—was now an important element in our budget, it was on the price we got for our stock that our futures ultimately depended.

By the time I had dealt with William, dawn had broken. It was a grey misty day with a slight drizzle seeping through the trees. Beneath the depressing skies the mole-infested lawn was more of a mess than ever. Criss-crossing its length were great weals of dead grass, the roots of which had been removed during the tunnelling. At intervals along these scars were little humps of earth. I tried to ignore the scene. I must stop thinking that these moles are a bad omen, I told myself sternly.

As usual for a market day, both Tom and I were on edge. We knew the market had dropped back from its summer peak, now that the autumn flush of cattle was coming into the auction ring. But the government had raised the floor price for fat cattle by ten per cent the previous spring, so we hoped we would make about ten per cent more than we had the year before.

I hurried to get the guests' breakfast cooked and the washing-up done, while Tom did the chores outside and called the cattle into the farmyard ready to load. We chased the dozen heifers we were selling up the ramp into the lorry, and Tom departed in it with Anthony. I followed half an hour later in the car with William.

Trying to find your husband between rows and rows of cattle pens when the only distinguishing feature you can make out is his hat, is always a difficult job, but after ten minutes combing the maze of pens I found Tom. He was looking particularly pleased with himself.

"The cattle are down here." He led the way through the iron pens. We reached a pen in which stood some cattle which looked rather like ours, but which had a blue card tied onto the rails indicating that they had won a prize in the show preceding the auction. I looked again. They were our cattle. I hugged Tom. We had been awarded second prize for the best store cattle over eighteen months. It may have been only a market show, but to us it meant more than an award at Smithfield. Equally important, it meant we should be bid a good price for them.

We took our seats in the empty ring and slowly the auction came to life, like a theatre stirring for a performance. First the bell was rung. The lights went on, then came the performers—the auctioneers in white coats like psychiatric attendants. Finally, in shuffled the public. At first it was difficult to judge how prices were faring, because the sale started with the ill-sorted lots—cows and calves, single animals, barren Friesian heifers. Then came several bunches of heifers similar to ours. I heard the prices in amazement. The market had not just dropped, it had fallen through the floor. Prices were much the same as the previous year and the year before that—£30 a hundredweight. Inflation had pushed up all our costs, but had, it seemed, left our prices untouched. Not again, I thought; it cannot happen again. Surely once again we have not got all those Irish cattle flooding into the country, receiving a subsidy of £15 a hundredweight.

Our cattle came into the ring.

"£250," called the auctioneer. No takers.

"£230."

"Come on, then, £220."

"All right, then, £200 to start."

With every call my spirits sank lower. Then the bidding was under way.

"£205; £210; £220."

Then the bids edged up a pound at a time. I set my teeth. There was no brucellosis test to complicate the sale of our cattle this year, to make it difficult for us to take them back unsold. Yet it is extraordinarily difficult to withdraw cattle from a sale. Every fibre of your body urges you to sell them. That is the object of the whole exercise. Tom, who is hopeless at mental arithmetic and detests metrication, was standing in the auctioneer's box looking towards me for my signal. I shook my head angrily. The auctioneer closed the bidding. "Lot withdrawn," he said.

When I met Tom outside the sale ring we both cursed our luck. Yet we did not feel the same impotent helplessness that we had felt the year before. We could afford to fight back now. We did not have to have cash then and there. The farm holidays had given us an invaluable margin of ready money. We would take the cattle back home and hang on until the price improved.

"It's no good," Tom and I agreed. "Those cattle have got to make £32 a hundredweight. And that's not asking too much. Lots of people have been counting on £40 a hundredweight, otherwise we have just thrown away all the winter feed we have put into them, to say nothing of our work."

"We've still got plenty of grass anyway. Let's hope the weather doesn't turn cold."

As I helped Tom to load the cattle back on to the lorry a voice called out: "Are those yours?"

"Yes. We're taking them home."

"No good, is it?"

The speaker was a small elderly man in a brown overall. His eyes were glazed with anxiety; another luckless farmer who had felt the pressure to sell and had resisted.

"Hopeless," I confirmed. "These took second prize in the show and we were only bid £30 a hundredweight for them."

He nodded, reassured. "It's been just a day out for mine. Fifteen minutes in the market and back into the meadow. My ten hundredweight cattle made less than £300. I can get £315 for them from the slaughterhouse and get out of paying £15 commission to this lot."

I drove on ahead with William and, once back at Deerpark, started to shovel his lunch into him.

About fifteen minutes later Tom arrived back in the lorry. He whistled to me to help him lower the ramp.

The accident happened in a matter of seconds. As Tom opened the first gate at the top of the ramp the cattle surged out. (The wooden gates not only kept the cattle inside the lorry, but when the ramp was lowered they swung aside to form a set of banisters down the side of the ramp.) Both Tom and I leapt clear of the stampeding cattle. They were all clear except one beast.

"You all right?" asked Tom. I assured him I was. "Nip up to the loft and get a sack then. This heifer's caught her foot."

I collected a sack and gave it to Tom. He put it under the heifer's foot and tried to lever it free.

"Get behind her and push her forward," he ordered.

Only then, as I put my weight behind the animal, did I realise the seriousness of the heifer's predicament. As she had hurtled down the ramp her foot had slipped off the edge at a point unguarded by the wooden gate. She was trapped between the ramp and the spring that attached the ramp to the lorry. Her other three feet were on the ground, but this one back foot was jammed. The joint was twisted and still firmly wedged. I pushed against her and Tom tried to push the foot free again. All the time the task was getting more and more difficult as the joint was swelling up. We tried again.

Seven hundredweight of heifer is a huge weight to manoeuvre. After about three minutes of heaving and pushing a sense of stalemate crept over us. Our cherished prize-winning heifer was hopelessly stuck.

"Keep propping her up," said Tom, striding off towards the house. "We're going to need help. I'll phone John Hopkins."

From the kitchen I could hear William, strapped into his high chair and abandoned in the middle of lunch, screaming and screaming. Suddenly the heifer lent her full weight on me. I pushed against her. I must stop her falling, I thought desperately, there's only me between her and . . . I could not bear the thought of it. But I could not hold her. Slowly she slumped to the ground, her foot still caught. Squeamishness is not one of my failings, but nor have I the phlegmatic nature of a doctor, a nurse or a vet. I looked at the heifer and screamed.

"Tom! Tom! Oh, my God, Tom! Get somebody! Get the slaughterhouse!"

Behind me Anthony was watching the whole macabre drama. A piping voice asked: "What's the matter, Mummy? Heifer's leg's broken, innit?" Then he added soothingly, "Don't shout."

What sort of effect will this ghastly business have on my son's development, I wondered?

To our relief John Hopkin's van shot into the yard within a matter of minutes. He glanced at the heifer. "I should phone Phil Lewis if I were you. The slaughterhouse won't give you what she's worth, so you may as well have the meat for your own freezer."

"We can't leave the poor thing like this," said Tom, who had been helping me to support her. "There's only one thing we can do. I'll get the hacksaw from the toolshed."

I took the cowardly way out and went into the house with John Hopkins, who was to phone Phil Lewis. Not for the first time I blessed our luck in living in a part of Britain which still retained its traditional rural skills. At least there were still local butchers who knew how to slaugher animals in a farmyard or in a barn.

Fifteen minutes later Phil's little green van bounced up the drive. Never had anyone been more welcome at Deerpark. With his bright smiling face he was everyone's idea of a cheery family butcher. But he also had an air of quiet authority. He took over, assigning jobs to Tom and John. Calmly and methodically, as if he did it every day of his life, he slaughtered the heifer. On a gritty farmyard with no proper blocks or pulley, with only the front loader of the tractor as a hoist, he dealt with the heifer with the same rhythmic skill he used in a slaughterhouse. There was not a spot of dirt on the carcase. He had reduced the chaotic messy disaster to a clean kill. A real craftsman.

Afterwards he brought the offal into the kitchen. I had never been particularly keen on beef offal, so I asked his advice.

"What do I do with the heart?"

"That's 'Poor Man's Goose'. Boil it for an hour, then stuff it and roast it."

I looked at him in disbelief. People eating squirrel was one thing. But in Herefordshire of all counties surely ox heart could not masquerade as goose?

"It is," Phil assured me. "In the old days when we butchers killed our own cattle for the shop the hotels in town used to take all the ox hearts we had at Christmas. If you carve them properly they look and taste just like goose. When you think about it there isn't a lot of meat on a goose. A hotel feeding a lot of people at Christmas couldn't possibly cook enough geese to feed all of them."

Outside Tom and John were sweeping the blood off the farmyard. Out of sight in the barn hanging from the front loader of the tractor was the carcase of the luckless heifer. I looked at the clock. Five o'clock. The guests would be back for supper any minute but all trace of the disaster had been removed.

"Don't say a word to them," warned Tom. "It could spoil their holiday."

We had reckoned without Anthony. As soon as the guests stepped out of their car half an hour later, he ran breathlessly to meet them.

"Heifer's broken its leg. Ramp fell down and heifer caught its leg in the hinge. Phil killed it and it's in the barn."

"What's all this about?" asked the woman, greatly puzzled. "Anthony says a heifer is dead."

"No. No, I don't know what he's on about." Tom was dismissive. "Children talk a lot of nonsense at his age."

We went into the house and poured ourselves two large tumblers of lettuce wine.

Over the months that followed we had little chance of forgetting the whole horrifying experience. To Anthony it was the most momentous event he had ever witnessed. For weeks afterwards he would lift up the receiver of his toy telephone, known as the 'hot line', and retell the story to his grandfather, to John Hopkins and to various aunts and uncles. As time went by it was enshrined in a chant that was recited in the same rhythm as Jack and Jill:

Gate fell down,
And heifer broke its leg,
And Phil came out and killed it.

At other times he would walk round the farm pointing
at various animals saying: "That pussy's not broke its
leg," or "That heifer's not got a broken leg." Sometimes
when we sat down to a meal of stew or liver he would say
disarmingly: "Dat's de heifer, innit?" Yet the incident
did not haunt him. He had known death ever since he had
begun to comprehend the world around him. He had
seen birds shot for food and the bodies of our cats that had
died in mysterious circumstances. To him death was as
natural as the birth of kittens, as eggs hatching or a cow
calving, all an integral part of the cycle of our life of the
land. I envied him his equanimity.

There was a chill in the air now that made us catch our
breath and quicken our steps when we nipped coatless
out of the door, and into the yard. Skies, deep and clear
for so many weeks began to fill with dusty clouds.
Hedgerows were turned prematurely bare as the
mechanical hedgecutters mercilessly wacked the leaves
and twigs off them. Yellow fields were stripped of stubble
as ploughs carved up the rich earth.

At the end of the first week of October the last visitors'
car chugged down the drive. We waved them goodbye
with mixed feelings.

My first reaction was that I would be able to catch up
on some sleep. I had stayed the course, but only just. I felt
weary in every corner of my being, and my hair had
started to fall out in handfuls. I felt that I could not have
cooked one more breakfast or washed up one more set of
dishes. Yet I felt too a pang of regret. I had become used
to the bustle and the company of the guests. Now the
winter loomed ahead long and lonely. So with relief
tinged with sadness I rearranged the furniture to make

Deerpark our home again. Blankets were folded up and put ready to wash before the weather became too damp to dry things on the line. Our clothes, that had been stuffed into suitcases and boxes for the summer, were aired and put back into drawers and wardrobes.

But still the fine weather held. Autumn days were banished again by a determined sun conquering the clouds. Warm soft air enveloped us. The vegetable garden continued to behave as if it was late August, producing barrowfuls of beans, tomatoes and courgettes. Each of the seed potatoes I had planted yielded about five pounds of potatoes complete with a bumper crop of slugs. Cabbage-white butterflies were still laying eggs, and caterpillars were hatching as fast as we sprayed the plants against them and their voracious appetites.

Splashes of yellow suddenly appeared in the ring of trees that bordered the farm. Then small groups of trees in the wall of green foliage burst into a flaming glory of gold and bronze as if ignited at random by some unseen hand.

This fine weather brought out the tourists again. They, too, proved to be a late crop. With school half-term the phone rang. Could we manage a booking for four? We were plummeted back into the guest-house business. Blankets were hurriedly dried in front of the Aga, beds rearranged, all our clothes packed away again. Food was replenished from the market. It was a lot of work, but I was fresh and fit again now, and it was worth the trouble, even if the guests were with us for only one week.

When they left, the season was finally over. It was eighteen months since the Prices' Marina had made its way gingerly up our roadway. They had been eighteen hard, hard months, complicated by the unexpected arrival of William in our midst. But they had been months in which we had turned a corner. Our earnings from the guests had provided us with the margin that had not only managed to keep us in the black, but had enabled us to make a modest further investment for the future.

In the last of those sunny autumn days before the winter came howling and roaring and crackling in, we had in our barns and pens and fields the living proof that our holiday venture had been worth all its toil, tears and sweat.

The market had picked up as Christmas loomed near and we had sold forty head of cattle at a reasonable price. This had paid off last year's overdraft and had left us with part of our next year's stock already in hand. The paying guests had not just kept the wolf from the door for eighteen months, they had enabled us to increase the number of animals we were carrying on the farm. Looking around at the extra calves and horses in the pens and boxes in the farmyard, I tried to work out how many nights of bed, breakfast and evening meals they represented. Hundreds and hundreds. And how many souvenir jars of jam and pots of tea had we sold to pay for their feed?

Buffy, Bambi's black calf, stared affectionately at Tom from the pen by the barn. The Kentlands with their pyromaniac son had paid his keep for the year. With Buffy were three black and white heifer calves. Their winter feed costs would be neatly offset by the receipts from the friendly concert party quartet who had stayed at Deerpark in May. In the loosebox next to the pen were half a dozen baby calves. At least two of them were being maintained by the Maynards, who had liked their meat 'properly' cooked; the energetic family with the metal detector would maintain the others. Out in the meadow were four new Friesian heifers which we planned to sell at a good price to dairy farmers, for they would be good milkers. Perhaps it was fitting that the Blakeways, who proved some women still know their place, should have provided the money to keep these heifers for the coming year.

Four horses' heads now hung over the loose-box doors. Apart from Tom's old show jumper, all were newcomers. We had acquired a mare and a filly and the colt we hoped to register as a stallion.

In cash terms, therefore, the idea which had struck me that afternoon in the kitchen garden, had been a good one. And the cash alone had not been the only reward. Despite all the disappointments and, indeed, the humiliations, and above all, despite the pounding, slogging work, it had been, to a surprising degree, fun. We had met, entertained and made friends with a great many varied people and had learnt some fascinating things about their lives and jobs. We had been brought into touch and kept in touch with the world outside. Farming can be a lonely and thankless job. Livestock farming calls for unceasing attention to animals which depend upon you utterly for sustenance and care. And at the end of it all, the animals you have reared and tended and fattened are destined for the slaughterhouse. You do not remind yourself that this is what it is all about. You take a pride in looking after them well and producing good, strong, sleek beasts, which will not only fetch a good price, but which will have been healthy and contented. Farming is a life of long hours, hard manual labour, all for a slim margin of profit. At the end of it all your only thanks are likely to be a look of thankfulness (and surprise) from your bank manager and the irritation of hearing on the radio a whining spokesman for the consumers, earning his £10,000 a year by complaining about the way farmers are exploiting housewives.

The paying-guest business, on the other hand, not only gave us a reasonable profit, but gave us a sense that people appreciated our efforts and felt they were getting value for their money. It seems crazy economics that the production of essential foodstuffs such as beef and veal can be highly precarious, a process in which the outcome of all your work can be swept aside by one lurch of the market, whilst the provision of a valuable but less essential service, such as holidaying, can provide a steady if by no means rich return. But that is the way it is and we were thankful that events had enabled us to develop this second string to our highly-stretched bow.

Our holidaying venture has at least won for us a further period of survival as a small farm. And who knows whether the tide is not going to turn in favour of smallness in agriculture, and enable holdings of the size of Deerpark to prove that, far from being an anachronism, they are merely ahead of their time. We smallholders may be well fitted to survive in a world where energy supplies are diminishing fast and where economic growth is slowing down. The labour-intensive family farm, using muscle power as well as diesel fuel, muck as well as artificial fertiliser, re-cycling junk and scrap in its buildings and its machinery, could enjoy a revival.

With winter on us, I began to plan for the next summer. Already my memories were fading of the harrowing days when I was doing all the cooking between four-hourly feeds for the baby. I turned to Tom: "We could all move into the two rooms above the kitchen next year and decorate the boys' room for the guests. We could then book in more than one group at a time, since they don't seem to mind sharing a bathroom and they seem to like the company."

Tom agreed. "I've been telling you that for ages. People are like animals. They're miserable on their own."

My thoughts were running ahead. "We could turn the middle living room into a dining room for the guests. That means we would be upgraded by the Tourist Board . . ."

On the lawn the moles had stopped throwing up heaps of earth. Instead they were just making holes and occasionally ejecting the odd mothball on to the grass.

Perhaps they were attempting a policy of co-existence. Beyond the farm, over the Marches a cold mist was rising. To the north the rugged heights of Clee Hill were dark and brooding. To the west the Black Mountains and Brecon Beacons seemed to cower under thick skies, heavy with foreboding. Radnor Forest was a black smudge on the hills. Around the farm, the trees, their leaves turning quickly now, no longer looked gloriously autumnal; they seemed tired and spent. Suddenly the countryside felt inhospitable. The snow was coming.